THE
CHICANO
HERITAGE

A COMMUNITY SCHOOL IN A SPANISH-SPEAKING VILLAGE

L. S. TIREMAN

and

MARY WATSON

ARNO PRESS

A New York Times Company

New York — 1976

Editorial Supervision: LESLIE PARR

———◆———

Reprint Edition 1976 by Arno Press Inc.

Copyright © 1948 by the University
of New Mexico Press

Reprinted by permission of the
University of New Mexico Press

THE CHICANO HERITAGE
ISBN for complete set: 0-405-09480-9
See last pages of this volume for titles.

Manufactured in the United States of America

———◆———

Library of Congress Cataloging in Publication Data

Tireman, Loyd Spencer, 1896-
A community school in a Spanish-speaking village.

(The Chicano heritage)
Originally published in 1943 under title: La
comunidad.
Reprint of the ed. published by the University
of New Mexico Press, Albuquerque.
1. Nambe, N. M. Community School. 2. Educa-
tion--Experimental methods. I. Watson, Mary,
principal, Nambe School, joint author. II. Title.
III. Series.
LD7501.N172T5 1976   373.789'56   76-1596
ISBN 0-405-09527-9

A COMMUNITY SCHOOL IN A
SPANISH-SPEAKING VILLAGE

A COMMUNITY SCHOOL IN A SPANISH-SPEAKING VILLAGE

By

L. S. TIREMAN

*Professor of Education, University of New Mexico
and Director, Nambé School*

and

MARY WATSON

Principal, Nambé School

UNIVERSITY OF NEW MEXICO PRESS

ALBUQUERQUE : : 1948

Dedication

This book is dedicated to teachers
who are working with bilingual
children and sincerely attempting
to help them

Preface

This text, A COMMUNITY SCHOOL IN A SPANISH-SPEAKING VILLAGE, was originally published in 1943 under the title *La Comunidad.*

That title was selected because the main irrigation ditch in the little Spanish-speaking pueblo is called "La Comunidad." We hoped to suggest that as water is of supreme importance in a thirsty land so the school can make an equally significant contribution to the life of the people.

However since the title was in Spanish some people feared that the book was written in that language. So for this reprinting we forego the symbolic title for a more descriptive one.

L. S. T.

Acknowledgments

As director of the project, it is a privilege to express my personal thanks not only to those people who helped constantly with the school program but also to those who have helped with the planning, writing, and preparation of the manuscript. It is impossible to thank adequately all of the agencies and individuals who contributed so much to the program of the Nambé School. The staff is fully aware that our program would have been sadly handicapped without your generous assistance.

First, to the staff of the Nambé School I would like to express my appreciation and gratitude for their coöperation and excellent work in the classrooms and in the community; and to Mary Watson who, throughout the five years, was the heart of the project, without whom this particular report would not exist.

The part which Mr. and Mrs. Cyrus McCormick played is evident throughout the work. Their financial aid made the undertaking possible, their friendship and interest made them always our good neighbors. And it was through the efforts of Mrs. McCormick that the Nambé health clinic was established and a second nurse secured for Santa Fe County. Mr. and Mrs. Joseph Granito, of the County Education Department, stood by throughout the experiment.

Anne Raymond and Julia B. Tappan, of the Soil Conservation Service, gave consistent and generous advice and assistance from the beginning of the experiment to the final pub-
lishing of the report. My appreciation is given to Mr. Mus-
grave, of the Soil Conservation Service, for his guidance and
counsel; to Dr. Lathrop, of Santa Fe, who gave not only his
professional assistance but a sympathetic understanding and
treatment of health problems; to Miss Augustine Stoll, who
coöperated with the Nambé nurse and made possible the
continuation of the clinic. My thanks, also, to the following
individuals who helped with transportation, clothes, materials, and neighborly assistance: Mr. Henry Ortiz, Mr. and
Mrs. D. W. Campbell, Mr. Juan Rivera, Mr. and Mrs.
Walter Goodwin, Mr. Abel Ortiz, and Mr. Seferino Lujan.

It is unnecessary to say that the publication could not
have been written without the diaries, the accounts, and the
work of the staff. Those who have contributed specifically
to the manuscript are: Mr. McCormick, Miss Tappan, Miss
Raymond, Mr. Angel, Mrs. Sanchez, Mrs. Armijo, Mrs.
Ford, Miss Ortiz, Mrs. Jones, Miss Wyss, and Mrs. Maria
Casias Vergara. Miss Margaret Wyss, in particular, de-
serves my warmest thanks for her indefatigable help in
preparing the manuscript. The Soil Conservation Service
has supplied several of the pictures in the book.

The federal, state, and local agencies which constantly
took part in the program are here listed and their functions
described in the chapter on "Coöperation." But all agencies
are made up of individuals who by their thoughtful help
smoothed our path and strengthened the program: the

Board of Education of Santa Fe County; the General Education Board; the University of New Mexico; Mrs. John J. Kenney, county supervisor, NYA; the WPA, which assisted with our programs of music, crafts, recreation, hot lunch, and nursery school; the Forest Service; the Red Cross; the Soil Conservation Service; U. S. Children's Bureau; Veteran's Bureau; Mr. S. M. Ramirez, Santa Fe County agricultural agent; Mrs. Carlos Gilbert, Santa Fe County home demonstration agent; Dr. Frank Parker, Santa Fe County Health Department; Maternal Clinic, Santa Fe County; the Public Library, Santa Fe; the Catholic Clinic, Santa Fe; the New Mexico State Vocational Education Department; the New Mexico State Public Health Department; the New Mexico State Welfare Department; the New Mexico State Agricultural College; 4H Club Extension Service.

The staff over a period of five years included: Frank Angel (four years), Mrs. Celia Armijo (two and one-half years), Mrs. Terecita Olguin Baca (one year), Sue Brannon (one-half year), Mrs. Mayme Ford (three years), Mrs. Katherine Powers Gallegos (one year), Adelina Garcia (one-half year), Mrs. Jantha Hall Hampton (one year), Mrs. Ann Jones (two years), Mrs. Mary Little (two years), Pauline Mater (one year), Cordelia Ortiz (five years), Esther Pfiester (one year), Mrs. Georgia Reece (one year), Mrs. Victoria Sanchez (four years), Mrs. Maria Casias Vergara (two years), Anna Vigil (one year), Mrs. Mary Watson (five years), Dr. Velma Woods (two years), Margaret Wyss (two years).

L. S. TIREMAN, *Director.*

Table of Contents

List of Illustrations

Prologue

This, then, is the community . . .
The men who till the fields with hand plows and
thin horses,
The women who keep the homes—the land-softened
adobe homes . . .
The women with soft deep eyes that hold all the
pain and all
The strength of generations.
This, then, is the community . . .
The grandfathers who look like seers and saints
And can denounce the new ways as with the wrath
of God.
Or sit with children
Resting in the shadow of a wall.
The narrow strips of fields along the valley floor
Life-giving fertile spots amid the barren land
Watered and husbanded with care
For all these many years.
A hard place for a man to farm,
A hard place for a family to live,
But with a feeling and a strength that holds you
And calls you back.
This, then, is the community—
The houses huddled in the valley,

The gaunt church on the hill,
The road and the carts and the cars and the trucks,
The graveyard with its sunken graves and its crosses
And iris in the spring.
This, then, is the community? And is this all?
No, the community is not here—
Not in the roads, not in the fields,
And not under the roofs of the houses.
This is the community—
The feeling of people at prayer,
The feeling of people in misery, in doubt and
      insecurity.
This is the community—
The pride of people in their own—not alone their
      own houses,
Or their own fields, or their own horses,
But the pride of the community in their blood,
Their sons and their daughters—
And the future the sons and daughters may have.
This is the community—
The people rising together
To fight, to work, to pray.
The people laughing together, weeping together,
The people smiling on the road and in the homes—
The men singing as they leave the fields,
The children in the sun.
The people accepting death and tragedy,
The silent acceptance and the losing battle of two
      hundred people

Against a century of progress and of different ways.
The people together — at one with the crumbling
*   fields*
And the eroded pasture lands.
This is the community — the fears and the hopes
And the gladness and sadness
Of a hundred and a hundred years.

MARGARET WYSS

Chapter 1

The Nambé Community

Eighteen miles north of Santa Fe a twisting country road branches off the oiled highway and follows the Nambé River until it curves over a hill and down along the outskirts of the village. To the right of the road are the grounds of the school; beyond the school and above the road is the church. In the valley, level with the river, is the Nambé village proper with houses built along the three arroyos and along the banks of the river. Above the small, narrow fields, the orchards, and the adobe houses of the village rise the mountains of the Sangre de Cristo range. The shallow Nambé River winds through the fields and by the houses. Instead of one or two broad fields there are dozens of little fields, symmetrically marked off and planted in alfalfa, beans, corn, potatoes, peas, and chili. Fields run from the edge of the eroded arroyo banks to the very walls of the houses. Through the village runs one road, lined with heavy, old cottonwoods; rutted and packed from constant usage through the years, it crosses and recrosses the wide arroyos which extend to the river.

The village is old, founded in 1711 by one Gaspar Ortiz y Paiz, who came via ox-cart from Tampico, in old Mexico. The adobe house which he built still stands and many families in the village bear his name and are of his blood. The ditch which he built to bring the water from the river to the fields is still used by the villages. It is called "La Comunidad" and exists for the use of the community. The men use the ditch and care for it as they care for the church, the responsibility passing from generation to generation, from father to son. La Comunidad is symbolic of community life. Through the years it has been extended to more and more homes. In some generations and in some decades it has been full and carried life to all. In other times, it has been neglected and all have suffered. In the same way the church, the school, and other social institutions have been strong or weak as the people of the community sensed the need for them. When there is snow in the mountains and water in the river, the ditch flows swiftly and deep. There is water for all the small fields, and it is fairly distributed. In the spring, when the ditch is cleaned, the men send labor according to the amount of water they use. If a man irrigates three fields he may send three sons to aid in cleaning the ditch; if a man irrigates one field he may send only one son or come himself to help clear the ditch of silt and rubbish. The ditch is an example of an old community law of effort given and value received, a law which is valid only if all in the community accept its existence. It is the acceptance by the people of the village of responsibility toward its institutions and traditions that insures the strength of the community. As the people care for their ditches, their homes, and their church, they also care for their own people. La Comunidad — all of us.

Since the early eighteenth century a group of people have lived, worked, and died in the same community. Settling on the old Nambé Indian Pueblo grant the people lived peacefully with their Indian neighbors, irrigating their fertile land, grazing their small flocks and herds, using water from the river, cutting wood, building their adobe houses. There was land enough for all, fuel enough, grazing land or fodder enough for each family's needs, water enough for village and pueblo, wild game and fish. For many years they lived an isolated existence, first under the rule of Spain, then Mexico, and finally the United States, but still speaking the same language — Spanish — holding to the customs, the beliefs, the superstitions of seventeenth century Spain. The pattern of Nambé is very similar to the other Spanish-American towns in this part of New Mexico. There was plenty of land until about 1850.

The food crops were at that time supplemented by stock-raising in a modest way and by hunting, especially the annual buffalo-hunting expeditions. The Civil War touched the region only slightly, but it brought a market for livestock, and, more important, it introduced money into the economy. By 1875 the land was definitely overcrowded, and when the Denver & Rio Grande Railway built its spur from Alamosa, Colorado, to Santa Fe, it was a temporary solution. All the men who wanted work had it at $1 for a 12-hour day — unbelievably high wages for that day.

Thus was introduced the notion of wage work and cash income. Since then an ever increasing percentage of the **male** population has left the region to work in Colorado, Wyoming, Utah, and other parts of New Mexico as section-gang hands, miners, smelter workers, sheep herders, or as farm laborers. The World War merely accelerated the trend, and outside wages, which at one time were merely supplementary to the main source of livelihood, which was agriculture, now became the chief source. Up to 1929, on the average of one person per family went out to work for 4 to 7 months at wages varying from $40 to $100 per month. Since 1929 this source of income has progressively diminished, and today we find two or three working from communities that at that time sent out 100 to 150 people each year. The net result is that at the present time the relief load is between 60 and 70 per cent of the people of the area, and most of the people not receiving relief are indirectly depending for a livelihood upon relief orders.[1]

So today the old independence is gone. The impact of a modern industrial world, cash buying and selling, the development of commercial farming and stockraising, the increase of population, the loss or overuse of grazing land has left the people bewildered and at a low economic level.

The people still till their irrigated strips with care and, after more than two hundred years of continual use, the irrigated land is in surprisingly good condition, even though today they often use the same methods and the same hand-made tools of leather and wood used by their grandfathers.

Original farms have been divided and subdivided until today land holdings on the whole are small. The largest

---

[1] *Tewa Basin Study*, Volume II, Soil Conservation Service, Southwest Region, 1939, pp. v, vi.

holding in 1939 was sixty-five acres, the smallest, one and two acres. The average is about four or five, inadequate for even the subsistence needs of the family.

In past years overuse of grazing land up to the border of the national forest land on the Sangre de Cristo Mountains has severely taxed the watershed so that flash floods and run-off have denuded slopes, cut irrigated land, dumped silt and rubble.

True, the graciousness of the old ways of living still exists. There is much of the independence of spirit characteristic of people who have always lived close to the land, but in only a few families is there any stability or security. In general, there is poverty, apathy, and resignation. The village is in a period of transition and the solution is not easy. New ways of earning cash, new practices of land use, new ways of buying and selling, more land resources and water will have to be devised if the people are to find a secure place for themselves and their children in this changing world.

. . . Every family depends upon agriculture for its food supply, and most of the families have to depend upon it for their total income. As in the other communities in the area, the subsistence crops come first. Practically nowhere in the Tewa Basin — and Nambé is not the exception — is the land or the climate suited to wheat (with the exception of Truchas); and yet the people, in an attempt to escape the uncertainties of the market, continue year after year to devote a major portion of their meager land resources to this crop. At least a third of the land at Nambé is planted in wheat, and the yield varies from between 14 to 25 bushels per acre. Here, too, they use a variety of Red Durham wheat, and most of the crop is ground into flour locally. The cost of grinding at the water-mill is 10 per cent of the wheat for the owner of the mill. The mills of the region are ancient and crude. . . .

The other crops are the common ones in the area. There are some oats and considerable alfalfa. Every family has its garden plot, where they grow onions, chili, and other vegetables. These last are becoming increasingly important, as the people are taking up canning and preserving. Peas, aside from alfalfa, are the only nitrogenous crop; but this crop, although increasing in importance, is not yet significant. Nambé, apparently because of the protection furnished by the mountains to the east, is better fruit country than is the Pojoaque Valley further down; and this form of agriculture is becoming increasingly important. . . . Corn, the usual variety of Indian maize found in the area, is also common, and most of it is used for feed for the stock.

There are 12 looms in the community for the weavers who have learned weaving at the Santa Cruz High School, but there is no commercial weaving done. All of the weaving is done for home use, although it is of fair quality, and quite a large proportion is made of homespun. . . .

All the work on the ditches is done on a communal basis, and there is a tradition of mutual aid in certain kinds of work such as house building, planting, or harvesting. . . .

All the land farmed at Nambé is irrigated land, and the land held by the people is all under 3 long ditches out of the Pojoaque River to the north. All but 5 of the heads of families own land. . . . The three most important ditches from east to west are the El Llano Frio ditch, the La Comunidad ditch, and the Ortiz ditch. The first has 45 landholdings under it; the second and longest has 66 landholdings; and the third has 43. A few, notably Mr. McCormick, have land under the El Cano ditch. The land is fertile, and there is more terracing done to prevent erosion than elsewhere in the region.

Although Nambé is nearest the source of the Pojoaque River, and therefore has the first chance at the water supply, nevertheless there has been a dearth of water for irrigation since 1932. The people have made arrangements with the people of Pojoaque and San Ildefonso to use the water only 3 days per week, and allow it to flow down to the lower communities the other 4 days. The Nambé Indians have not come into this arrangement, but they have been considerate in allowing water to flow down the river below their ditches. The people of Pojoaque and San Ildefonso accuse the people of Nambé of being wasteful of water. The reason is that the Nambé people have constructed reservoirs, and they turn the water into these reservoirs when they no longer have need of irrigation. Because of this the Nambé farmers have had the best supply of water in the region, but even they had only enough water for one thorough irrigation in 1934.

The people here are dirt farmers and not stockraisers. This in recent years may be explained by the fact that the grazing land available has been practically ruined, and more recently the decisions of the Indian Pueblo Land Board have forced the Spanish people to keep all stock off the Pueblo lands. The total number of cattle does not exceed two hundred, and there is about an equal number of horses. . . . There are several small herds of goats, and every family has its flock of hens and a pig or two. Meat as an item of diet has been decreasing in importance in recent years, for obvious reasons, and will undoubtedly continue to do so in the future. The stock as it is everywhere in the region, is poor in quality, and it might be reasonably said that unless it is improved, it is as much a liability as an asset.[2]

The present Spanish-speaking population of the village is composed of 600 persons representing 160 families. There

2 *Ibid.*, pp. 2, 3, 4, 5, 6.

are eight English-speaking families living in Nambé. With the exception of Mr. and Mrs. McCormick, these Anglo families have bought property and built homes within the last four years.

The Spanish families generally consist of the parents and five to eight children, with often an older relative living with them. They are housed in two to five-roomed adobe houses. The home may be poor but there are always plants in the windows and a few pictures, either photographs or magazine illustrations, on the walls.

In Nambé there are several private businesses which are carried on by members of the community in addition to their farming. The oldest and most permanent is the flour mill, where much of the wheat and corn is ground into meal or flour by power supplied by an old overshot water wheel. There are four grocery stores, each carrying a limited supply of staple foods, one garage where cars are repaired and little gas is sold because the owner operates on a cash basis. One saloon has been established during the last two years, and here business proceeds regardless of the stipulated cash basis. There is a Catholic Church in the village, served by a priest who comes every other Sunday at nine o'clock to say mass. There is a lodge for men called "Sociedad Protectivo Mutual de Trabajadores Unidos" (S.P.M.D.T.U.) — United Brotherhood of Laborers. The membership is not large as the dues are high, including, however, insurance benefits. Each November the lodge celebrates the anniversary of its founding, and the celebration is something of

a feast day, with the church, the school, and the members
of the community participating.

THE ESTABLISHMENT OF THE COMMUNITY SCHOOL

The groundwork for a community school in Nambé was
laid when Mr. and Mrs. Cyrus McCormick bought the site
of the Nambé School as part of their property, and in payment gave a new piece of land and $1,000 toward a new
school building nearer the road. The two Nambé schools
were consolidated and in the winter of 1933-34 a second
building for the school was planned and built. The amount
of needed cash was contributed by the McCormicks, the
community put in labor as its share — and the poorer men
were paid by government relief. The second school building was not finished until three years later, when another
community effort was organized and cement was contributed by the McCormicks; 150 families contributed labor,
and the hall and porch steps were finished.

But Mr. McCormick was not satisfied. The new school
in itself did not seem adequate for the needs of the community. The villagers were not making full use of the
opportunities America offers. He knew there were people
who could teach the villagers new methods of agriculture
and help them to improve their living conditions; but the
villagers were not aware of their needs. Mr. McCormick
knew he could not bring these opportunities to the people
by himself. He knew that things such as these could not be
given as gifts. The only way for the people to find and build
the security they needed lay through their own realization

of their needs and their own efforts to obtain them. He wondered why the school could not help the people meet their needs. And, as he listened to the men and women sing as they plastered their homes and learned the wisdom of many of their ways, he realized that these people, if they were given a chance, had much to give toward the education of their children and the needs of their country.

In the spring of 1937 Mr. and Mrs. McCormick approached the University of New Mexico regarding the school in the community. They reported that they believed Nambé ready for a community school project based upon community coöperation. They expressed grave concern about the kind of education the children were receiving, and asked if there wasn't some way to bring a more practical program to them. In subsequent conferences between Mr. and Mrs. McCormick, Mr. Joseph Granito, Santa Fe County superintendent of schools, and Dr. L. S. Tireman, of the College of Education of the University, the possibility developed that it might be possible to adjust the curriculum of the school to better fit the needs of the people and the children.

Mr. Granito, representing the Santa Fe County Board of Education, agreed to coöperate in selecting teachers who would be interested in such a program and to give the school a free hand in making such curriculum changes as seemed desirable. Mr. and Mrs. McCormick agreed to supplement the county budget for the school with an annual subsidy for five years so no additional burden would be thrown on the taxpayers. The University designated Dr.

Tireman as director, and requested the General Education Board to allocate to the Nambé Project the unused remainder of a grant originally made to the San José Project.[3]

Mr. McCormick discussed the matter with citizens of Nambé and it was decided that a mass meeting should be held where the matter would be explained to the people and their coöperation solicited. If they said "no," it was agreed to drop the whole matter. During the ensuing days, it developed that many of the people were not satisfied with the school as it was then being administered. They felt that their children were not receiving the kind of education that was of value to them. This criticism was directed not so much at the teachers who were there as to the content which the children were required to learn. Superintendent Granito and Mr. McCormick had many conferences with individuals in the community. Such was the confidence of the people in the judgment of these two friends of Nambé, that at the mass meeting of the citizens the majority voted to try the new proposal, though a few were frankly skeptical.

SELECTION OF THE STAFF

The problem that faced the county superintendent and the director was the assembling of a staff who would be open-minded, familiar, and sympathetic with the problems of Spanish-speaking children; who were familiar with rural areas and endowed with the vision and experience which would be necessary for the realization of the aims of the project. Members of the staff were requested to live in the

---

[3] A former experimental school directed by the University.

community, for a community school would have been impossible with a commuting staff. While one of the stipulated requirements was experience, it was borne out in the following years that past experience was not nearly as important as the attitude of the teacher. The most important position to fill was that of principal. The director felt that the community should regard the principal as the leader and not be given any opportunity to go over her head to the director.

Chapter 2

Curriculum vs. the Child

Many centuries ago, according to legend, an old robber by the name of Procrustes lived by a ford in a river. As there was no other crossing place for a long distance, his armed forces took toll from every traveler who wished to pass the river. If the wayfarer was so unlucky as to be unable to pay, he was lodged in one of the dungeons of the castle and slept on the famous beds of Procrustes. These beds became notorious because Procrustes had a most ingenious way of fitting them to the needs of every sleeper. If the sleeper was too long and his feet stuck out, the soldiers would lop off enough of projecting parts to fit the owner to the bed. If the sleeper was too short, the soldiers attached cords to head and feet and stretched the unfortunate individual till he was long enough to fit the bed. In every case the traveler was made to fit the bed.

Without much strain on the imagination, this story can be retold today, substituting the word curriculum for the bed of Procrustes. The child is forced to go to school. Awaiting him is a fixed curriculum. He must learn to read in certain grades, cipher in others, and become acquainted

with geography and history in advanced grades. If he fits
into the accepted scheme, well and good. He progresses,
year by year, in a routine manner, passes into high school,
from there to college and ultimately graduates as an educated man or woman. But woe to the unfortunate one who
fails to fit into this orderly and mechanical pattern. If he
has greater natural capacity or is more advanced than his
classmates, he may "skip" a grade, but the chances are 100
to 1 that he will remain here performing piffling tasks
which afford no challenge or stimulation. The teacher will
not call upon him in the recitation because he knows all the
answers and she must give her attention to the failures!
He learns to "pull his punches" and to do no more than is
necessary. Schooling is a bore from which he cannot escape.
After ten to fifteen years of continuous restraint he has lost
all desire to exert himself for the sheer joy of achievement.
He does quite well what he is required to do, but the ambi-
tion to conquer the unknown, to utilize to the full his
powers, has been dulled. In truth, he has been lopped off
to fit the Procrustean bed.

At the other end of the group can be seen other misfits in
this lock-step-chain-gang called a class. Because of heredity
factors the child does not possess those abilities which are
necessary for academic achievement. He does not learn
quickly from books. He may be at home on the playground
or fields, he may be a fair workman with his hands, but ab-
stract knowledge is not his portion. Yet he is forced to sit
long hours and weary weeks while the teacher attempts to
"larn" him. The words of the reader are meaningless for

his concepts are vague and incomplete. He is in an intellectual fog! Occasionally a story impinges upon his experience and the light of understanding momentarily illuminates his drab life. Occasionally the teacher talks to him in a language he understands; once in a while there is some school activity wherein he may be permitted to take some small part. From these brief interludes he derives some benefit. But for the greater part of the time, he sits inert and uncomprehending while the classes go on about him.

The conscientious teacher gives him some attention but it is expected that a certain per cent will fail. "That is natural" and no criticism is attached to her when four or five "dumb" children are retained for a second year in the grade. Is this not a case of stretching the "short one" to fit the curriculum?

The Spanish-speaking children present an exaggerated situation. The curriculum now followed in New Mexico was originally designed for English-speaking children of the Atlantic seacoast. When the settlers from the East and Middle West came to make their homes in the Southwest, they brought their school along as naturally as they brought the right to worship as they pleased. The curriculum was based on the accepted principle that all children should go to high school and college. Very few thought differently and it was rather a social disgrace for the family if the children did not finish secondary school. Accordingly, the curriculum stressed academic requirements. One must learn to read not primarily to form intelligent opinions but to understand the history and literature courses. One learned to figure in order to do compound interest and complicated problems in algebra and geometry, not to fulfill the simple needs of everyday life. One studied language, not to perfect the art of speaking but to learn to write correctly and to understand the grammar. All of these accomplishments were useful to the child who would "go on" to high school and college. But the Spanish-speaking people of New Mexico had no such body of accepted principles. Education has never been the prerogative of the common people in Spanish-speaking countries. In a pastoral civilization the need for advanced education was not recognized. It was sufficient that a few possessed literary skills.

When the United States formally acquired this territory, it showed the most appalling lack of understanding. Political rights peculiar to a democratic people were conferred upon a people conditioned to aristocratic institutions. The United States Government made no effort to prepare the people to understand and accept this radical change in ideals and *mores*. By a stroke of the pen it was expected that a whole population would suddenly change its ways of living and thinking.

This statement could be documented in countless ways. The system of landholdings was suddenly changed from royal, tax-free grants to one requiring annual taxes. A social system founded upon caste was discarded overnight for a social system built upon freedom and equality. A monarchial government of kings and viceroys was replaced by an electoral system. In other acquired territories, the American government has realized the necessity of informing the new citizens and has utilized the schools in an attempt to teach American institutions. They have sent teachers, doctors, and sanitation experts, but in New Mexico the two different ideologies were permitted to run into each other headlong and nature allowed to take its course.

Only one answer was natural: to the victor belong the spoils. The Spanish-speaking people were expected to adjust themselves to the American pattern. They must learn English, they must learn to help run the government, they must educate their children because democracy rests upon a literate electorate. When soberly viewed from a historical perspective, it is rather remarkable that New Mexico has accomplished so much. Yet the appalling fact is that the common school has helped very little. Good roads, not education, have opened up the backward countries. In the main, county agents have advised the farmers and not agricultural departments in our common schools. Hard-pressed county nurses have struggled against ignorance and superstition regarding disease and the common school has given little aid. Hot lunches through government grants have done what the common school might have attempted. The Soil Conservation Service is saving the land, and sometimes the school ground, while the curriculum often omits the subject.

It is not recognized and honestly acknowledged that the curriculum could be and is an instrument of society and should be designed to do whatever needs to be done for the good of all. In other words, if New Mexico has problems which differ from the problems of New England, then the curriculum of the common school should be designed to aid New Mexico in the solution of its problems. It can *only aid,* for the school is but one *servant of democracy.* Quite unfairly, people are prone to expect the school to correct every evil. The school can do more than it has done, but it cannot do all. For example, it is strategically situated to coördinate the efforts of the many agencies existing to improve our commonwealth, but it cannot do their task.

The curriculum then, as a fixed Procrustean bed to which all must conform, has been a lamentable fixture of the common school. Wise teachers have long known that this idea must be changed. The Procrustean bed must be made adjustable to the child. The curriculum must be made to fit the needs of the child.

Most of the best administrators and best teachers of our New Mexico public schools would readily admit the truth of the above argument. They would point out, quite fairly, that they are ready to make changes but (1) the institutions of higher learning demand certain prerequisites and if the students who seek admission fail to possess them, the school is severely criticized by the parents, (2) teachers are trained along conventional lines by our teacher-education institutions, and (3) all adjustments of the curriculum call for greater budgets with the taxpayer suspicious of new fangled ideas.

The administrator says to the theorist, "Show us by actual demonstration a successful attempt to solve the conditions you describe."

Chapter 3

Guiding Principles

It is axiomatic that the method of doing a thing is determined by the purpose in mind. Consequently, in the
Nambé staff meetings we spent considerable time trying
to clarify and state our general philosophy. At hand was a
detailed survey made by the Soil Conservation Service
showing ownership and kind of land, acreage of each farm,
members of the family. This information was supplemented
by the intimate knowledge of the teacher whose home was
in Nambé and from the continual visitation program of
the staff.

Believing that, in the final analysis, a democracy rests
upon the individuals who compose it, we asked, "What can
we do to help these children to become good citizens? Will
most of them go to college, will most move to town and
become skilled artisans, will the majority remain in Nambé
in agricultural work, or what?" No one knew the answer.
A few families did move to town each year. Two people
from Nambé were away in college; one or two families had
recently moved from town to the country. A few families

went to a nearby mining camp. But the majority of the people were quite likely to remain there as their parents had before them in spite of a lack of sufficient acreage. Consequently, we said quite frankly that our job is not to prepare these children for college but to live happier and more efficiently in this community.

OUR GENERAL PHILOSOPHY

A school should be the center of the community. It should be sensitive to the needs of the community and, in coöperation with the parents, plan a program that will make the best use of all available resources. Such an environment should stimulate pupils to engage in many activities. Through participating in planning, executing, and evaluating their work they will learn to think and to use the facts and tools of learning. They should find the school a vital place in which it is good to live.[4]

This was somewhat radical. "It should be sensitive to the needs of the community . . ." "We proposed to keep in mind what Nambé needed even if it was somewhat different from Santa Fe or other parts of the state." ". . . in coöperation with the parents plan a program. . . ." Yes, we would ask the fathers and mothers what they thought would be helpful. ". . . that will make the best use of available resources." The program must stay close to this locality. It must try to close the gap now existing between school and community. ". . . they will learn to think." Now we were getting somewhere. If boys and girls can learn to think they will be prepared for life no matter whether they

---

[4] This and following quotations from *Nambé—A Community School,* University of New Mexico Press, 1939.

spend it on the farm, at a desk, or before a machine. "They should find the school a vital place in which it is good to live." School must be attractive. Too frequently our rural schools are drab and colorless, dull and uninspiring, full of defeats and frustrations. No wonder that the pupils leave as soon as possible, carrying with them such memories that when they become parents they have little concern whether their children go to school or not. Above all, our pupils must enjoy life and be happy in our school.

PRINCIPLES OF SELECTION OF SUBJECT MATTER

The following principles attempted to anchor our general philosophy to the ground. They made the boys and girls who were living in Nambé the center. Everything was subordinated to that thought. The detailed teaching materials of the various grades were to be evolved from that central fact. The very actions of the staff and all our thinking were directed to that end.

I. We shall try to find out what is most needed in the lives of the people of this community and minister to that before all else.

The needs of the people who live in Nambé were placed above everything else. Health, infant mortality, social relationships, land management, craft work, recreation, command of oral English were the sort of problems that needed attention. These are fairly typical of the small rural communities in New Mexico. Yet, very little attention is given to them in the ordinary curriculum.

II. We shall constantly try to discover and utilize the resources of the community. The fields, arroyos, the homes, and the shops shall be a part of our laboratories, and its workers numbered among our teachers.

If the school is to remain close to the community, it should use the resources that are there. By so doing, the curriculum becomes more meaningful for it deals with the stuff that composes the life of the community. Moreover, the competence of men and women of the community is recognized by seeking their help and contributions.

III. We shall utilize the service of all available agencies of the state which other rural schools can secure.

There are many county, state, and federal agencies with capable personnel who are eager to assist the schools. But the work must be coördinated and directed. The school must take the initiative in seeking aid, for frequently the people do not know how, or are too busy, to make the contacts. The school acts as a liaison agent.

IV. The starting point in every part of the curriculum will be Nambé. The pupil may go to the farthest point of the earth but he must follow the plan of going from something that is familiar and well known to something that is over the horizon. Unless that connection can be established by the pupils, we will relentlessly omit that part of the curriculum no matter how sanctified it may be by tradition and academic respectability.

This is only the application of an old principle, "start with the familiar and go to the unknown." If one honestly and consistently follows it, the formal and familiar course of study is subjected to rough treatment. Whole sections of organized knowledge rendered sacred by long use are omitted! This method places a premium on social utility and removes "knowledge for its own sake" to a secondary place. We doubted if we could follow the principle literally for we were a county school using the ordinary tests and subject to the county eighth grade examination, but we accepted the principle as a guide.

V. We shall not attempt to teach everything. If we follow points one and two, it means that more time will be needed to develop certain areas of experience than is customarily given.

Anyone who has worked on the curriculum knows that whenever new material is added, other material is crowded out or receives less attention. It is very difficult to exclude anything (1) which has once attained a favorable position; (2) the content of which was once highly useful and needed.

Since our surveys had indicated points of greatest need, we decided to emphasize health and land management. Throughout the various grades we would attempt to impregnate the regular subjects with concepts from these two fields. Thus, as far as we could, we would use reading materials which discussed these topics. Our social science work was centered around their ramification, e. g., relation of the proper use of land to prosperity of "all of us"; the effect of a good health program upon "La comunidad." Some of our arithmetic problems could deal with actual problems in Nambé.

VI. We shall expect each child to be reasonably proficient in the basic skills of the three R's and use English effectively. In addition we hope he can read as well as speak Spanish.

Again we tried to be realistic. A considerable number of our group were already so retarded in school work that they would be unable to go to high school and do the kind of work that our neighboring high school emphasized. We would accept them at their actual level and carry them as far as we would naturally. It seemed more important for the future of Nambé to have the big boys and girls happy in school, learning a little and acquiring right attitudes, than to try to run the risk of driving them out of school by high pressure methods designed to teach them information and skills which they could neither use nor understand.

We felt that the program we proposed would afford sufficient opportunity for the children with better ability to acquire necessary information and skills. Time alone would tell whether we were right and our eighth grade graduates could hold their own when they entered the ninth year.

In making such a decision we were influenced by our conviction that it is a mistake to expect the elementary school to teach all the skills or give all the information. The secondary school must also be held responsible for improving the basic skills through constant practice and direct instruction. To be concrete, the high school teacher must teach the pupil to read history as well as master the content.

". . . use of English effectively." It is extremely important that all children of Spanish-speaking descent become proficient in English. For those going to high school, the need is apparent. But we held that it was also extremely important that the boys and girls who did not continue in school should also speak good English. If Spanish had been the only language of Nambé and the only language of the people who dealt with the citizens of Nambé, then to be consistent we should have had to stress Spanish, but such is not the case. Outside contacts are in English, most of the available reading material is in English, employment is often affected by proficiency in oral speech. And of even more fundamental importance, we believe that the self-respect and self-confidence of non-English-speaking people is partially determined by their ability to meet their English - speaking friends and talk in English without marked accent and many errors. Personally, the writers are sure that their self-confidence suffers when in a foreign-speaking country they are prevented from free intercourse with people of social and professional station, because of poor language facilities.

We hoped that our pupils would be helped to "read as well as speak Spanish." This seemed desirable. Parenthetically, we were not successful in this respect. One of our staff who speaks excellent Spanish attempted to give instruction in that language, but the parents objected. They felt that the children had not yet learned English sufficiently so that time and emphasis could profitably be taken from it.

VII. We shall allow the pupils sufficient time for planning, discussing, experimenting, thinking.

The program we are discussing takes far more time than a formal program. It is much easier and shorter to assign a few pages in a certain text than it is to stimulate the pupils to raise worthwhile questions and then search for the answers. The former program necessitates understanding and subtly stresses acceptance. The latter program necessitates the additional steps of inquiry and evaluation. Evidences must be considered, lengthy discussions ensue, further search or experimentation may be required. All of this takes time and unless you allow time in your program, these things will not receive emphasis.

> VIII. Since we are aware that certain commonly accepted areas of school experience may be omitted, we will arrange reading lists so that the students may acquire some of the knowledge by themselves.

The principle acknowledges the possibility that the pupils who planned to go to high school might find themselves without certain conventional knowledge. Since this information is the most readily accessible material we have, it seemed possible for the pupil to acquire some of it by himself. The amount of forgetting is so great anyway, that probably most eighth graders would not appear very superior to our children! The county-wide eighth grade examinations would provide some check on the value of this principle.

> IX. The curriculum will be kept flexible so that units of work may be shifted to different levels to meet the interest and the ability of the various groups.

Freedom to adjust material is not only advisable but necessary. Groups of children vary from year to year in their abilities and interests. Unless the work be kept flexible it soon becomes as formalized as any other body of knowledge. Flexibility calls for careful management so that gradation in difficulty is provided and duplication avoided. The teachers must keep close together and know their children. This procedure emphasizes that the curriculum is a tool, a means by which boys and girls become educated. It is not an end in itself. It is to be used in the way best calculated to produce the results that the aim suggests.

Now the broad outlines of our answer to the traditional school begin to appear. Here was no bowing down to the familiar formal curriculum. Books no longer occupied the sole place in the learning process. Other means of learning were recognized. This school should not stand aloof, gathering its robes tightly about her to avoid the common touch. The education of the hand and the heart, as well as the brain, were recognized.

Chapter 4

Nambé Children at Work

INTRODUCTION

This chapter attempts to acquaint the reader with the actual program which was developed in the light of our principles to meet the needs of the Nambé children. The different sections were written by various members of the staff. Some of them are reports of a typical day, while others describe the general program followed for the year.

Since there are problems common to all grades, we have attempted to save too much repetition by mentioning them in this introduction rather than discussing them in each section.

1.   The children in the Nambé School, with the exception of three or four Anglos, came from Spanish-speaking homes. Most of the children knew no English when they entered school and many heard very little English outside the school. This situation is slowly changing.

2.   For various reasons, there was a large number of over-age children who were not scholastically equal to the demands of the grade in which their age would ordinarily find them.

3. Certain errors in oral English could be heard in every grade and demanded continual attention of the teachers.

4. The economic status of most of the parents was not high. Consequently, the breadth of experience of the children was limited. Specifically, a literary background was almost entirely lacking.

5. While the work was planned about large centers of interest, we did not follow an extreme activity program. There were scheduled periods for instruction in the regular school subjects.

6. The natural science program was not a special subject but was woven into the curriculum like a pattern in an old rug. It was definitely planned but might appear to the onlooker as a pleasing but accidental arrangement.

7. Visiting between rooms was common. This served to acquaint the pupils with the work going on at other levels.

8. New Mexico has a free textbook law. Supplementary books and materials were supplied by the project and a charge made of fifty cents per pupil.

THE PREFIRST ROOM [5]

The prefirst room is the most interesting room at school, in the opinion of many observers. Here are thirty-five little children who are in the process of learning English. And that is a difficult task. In the space of nine months the teacher must develop the vocabulary which an English-speaking child acquires before he goes to school.

The children sit on the floor in a big circle about the

___
[5] Written from the diary notes of Cordelia Ortiz.

teacher. Some shy, some bold, but all with shining, flashing eyes. What does the teacher have in the big package all wrapped up in white tissue paper? An ecstatic sigh escapes as she unwraps it. It is a big beautiful blue ————. No one knows the English word. They whisper excitedly among themselves and the teacher says, "This is a ball." They play with it, and they learn to say such sentences as, "I roll the ball," or "I throw the ball," or "I play with the ball. It is blue. It is big."

Some people might say, "They play all day!" If they mean that the children are wasting their time, they have failed to appreciate the significance of what they see. If they mean that the children go about their tasks in the happy but earnest spirit of play, it is true. The group in the playhouse is washing doll clothes, sweeping the floor, setting the table, with all the seriousness of real women in their own houses. As they work they gossip in true adult fashion about their tasks, but in English. If they do not know a word they turn to the teacher who is nearby to help them. The group over by the cupboard under the window is getting out the blocks. Presently you will see a house, a barn, a school or perhaps a church rising before your eyes. Play? Yes. But this play exercises judgment, choice, sharing, working together, all of which are pretty serious things in life.

The pattern breaks up as the teacher takes her accustomed seat in the circle. Blocks are quickly put back in the box, dishes are hastily stacked in the cupboard, the last dress is hurriedly pinned on the line and all the children gather at the feet of the "teecher." It is the magic story hour! It need not be described for we all have been enthralled by some story. The story must be told and retold, it must be dramatized, it must be played. And in the doing the ear becomes accustomed to the English sounds and the lips learn to use the English words in a natural manner.

Later, there are more formal periods when pictures are presented for description and discussion. Days may pass before some shy child will say a word in English. He is engrossed in trying to comprehend what the strange words mean. He is puzzled and confounded by the new language, for with all the patience of the teacher, with all the simplicity she can devise, the learning of a second language is very difficult for some children. But the day finally comes when the child points to some object or picture and names it. Wonderful! Magnificent! An achievement to be praised! Then must follow the many hours of practice. All the ingenuity of the teacher is taxed to keep these periods alive and purposeful. All her skill is needed to see that all the children participate, for they learn English by speaking English. When interest begins to lag the teacher leads in a rollicking singing game. "I put my right foot in, I put my right foot out, etc." and learning continues. Recess is only a change of classroom. Supervised play provides an excellent opportunity to use English under the stress and strain of competition. Frequently Spanish is used and that is natural. No one is scolded but he is praised when he can use English and the social approval of teacher and group is a powerful incentive to try to use English.

The approaching noon hour requires considerable preparation. The children must go to the toilet (which is not the simple matter it seems), they must wash hands and faces. When paper toweling is too expensive, the children are encouraged to bring clean cloths. A routine must be developed to care for all these duties, otherwise there is constant bickering. The tables are arranged, cups, plates, and spoons placed in position and the children learn to sit quietly and wait politely while the cocoa is poured and the hot food served. Juan does not like his dinner and cries for more familiar food. "All the other boys and girls like this, why don't you try it?" Soon he is asking for a second helping. "I want more beans, I dropped my napkin, I want more biscuits, thank you, you come after me, I like the dinner, excuse me," are the type of expressions heard.

After a morning of such vigorous mental and physical activity, the children curl up on rugs, or newspapers spread about the floor, and go to sleep. Those who won't sleep must be quiet and not disturb others and thus learn a lesson fully as important as English — self-control.

The program goes on day after day. Other objects, other pictures are presented, more and more conversation is carried on. Activities are encouraged which stimulate the use of the expanding vocabulary. The clever teacher utilizes many incidents to teach valuable lessons. Marie has a sore on her arm. Medicine is secured from the First Aid kit to treat it and Marie learns that more careful attention to cleanliness will help prevent a sore. A visit to the home by nurse or teacher is probably in order. "Marie is such a pretty girl and wears such nice clean dresses. It is too bad that she has this ugly sore. If you will do so and so, we think that Marie will not be bothered again."

The program for the year is centered around three large topics in the order mentioned.

School Acquaintance and Pets
   Schoolroom equipment
   Playground equipment
   Domestic animals and their care
   Rhymes and songs
Home
   Members of the family
   Parts of the body
   Clothes
   Foods
   Rooms and furnishings
Garden
   Learning the names of the seeds
   Names of equipment used for planting
   How to plant a garden
   Planting a garden

This arrangement teaches the English first needed in the fall and gradually extends out from the school room in conformity with our general principles. In the spring, the yard becomes a part of the room. The children have a small garden and they also follow with interest the work of the older children.

No one day adds a very appreciable amount to knowledge, habits, or skills. But, by the end of the year, the majority of the prefirst will know from 500 to 750 English

words. They will use English in the classroom, on the playground, and in many instances in the homes. They have
practiced health habits and they have learned to work together. They are looking forward with eagerness to the first
grade when they receive books and learn another magic
skill — to read English.

THE FIRST GRADE [6]

"May I have a book? When do we read out of a book?"
are the hopeful questions which the first-graders ask. Un-
fortunately, the answer is not simple nor easy. The forty-
two children are not a homogeneous group. A few have not
heard any English during the summer months and have
forgotten most of the English learned in the prefirst grade.
Others have remembered quite a bit but are slow in expressing themselves. They need more time and the stimulation of an English-speaking environment. The rest, however, gather confidently about the teacher, reaching for the
magic key to unlock the interesting worlds in the picture
books.

Knowing that there will be varied levels in the first grade,
the teacher has planned her equipment and materials to
meet their needs. There is a large box, on casters, full of
building blocks of different sizes. There is a huge wooden
chest full of odds and ends: toys, small utensils, but best of
all — dresses, hats, and slippers which will turn the little
girls into grown-up ladies or fairy princesses. There is a
terrarium with mosses, ferns, frogs, a salamander, and small

---

[6] Written from the diary of Mrs. Ford.

turtles. There is a game table, bulletin boards with pictures and beneath them little sentences which can't be read but certainly look interesting. And, of course, books are all about: big books with fascinating pictures; little books easy to hold, with short sentences which almost tell the story; shelves of books, and books from which the teacher reads enthralling stories. No wonder the children come early and sit on the doorstep waiting for the teacher or must be told, "Put away your books and go out to play. We will read again after recess."

But no matter how interested the children may be there is much hard work to be done before they begin to read. The boys and girls are encouraged to talk about their experiences at home, on the way to school, on the playground, and in the room. These oral stories are cleverly directed by the teacher in the interests of clarity, correctness, unity, and eventually emerge as group compositions which she writes (prints) on the blackboard. These are easy to read and, if skillfully made, lead the child by gradual steps to acquire an ability in English reading which eventually makes him able to read a preprimer or a primer. For example, the A group composed and read this chart:

Cooking

The girls made soup.
The boys brought vegetables.
We washed the vegetables.
We cooked the soup on the stove.
We ate the soup.
The girls liked the soup.

> The boys liked the soup.
> They said, "Thank you, girls."

The D (slow) group reads only simple experience charts such as this:

> We saw a brown rabbit.
> We saw a brown rabbit run.
> We can run.

By the middle of the year the A and B groups read primers and first readers while the slower groups have proceeded to more difficult charts or preprimers.

The oral English program of the prefirst grade is continued. Story-telling, dramatizations, directed conversation periods, and activities provide the opportunity for practicing English. The little girl in the first grade who had her impetigo healed forgot to be careful, or her mother was heedless, and her face was disfigured with scabs. Again the teacher must clean her up. Again the nurse or teacher must visit the home with sympathy because the conditions there are far from ideal, but with suggestions for improvement so that the little girl will not continue to suffer or the other children be endangered.

The hot lunch has worked wonders for several children. Some had been going without food at noon, others had only a cold tortilla. One child carried an empty pail every day so the other children would not know she had nothing. So both parents and children appreciated the lunch and sent donations.

The regular rest periods are continued. Some children tire easily because of malnutrition. Possibly some may find that the learning of a new language is mentally fatiguing. In any case, a rested child learns more easily.

The adjustment of the daily work to the individual needs of the children is nowhere better illustrated than in the many activities which the teacher plans for them. There are housekeeping duties, duties connected with the hand-washing, painting, clay modeling, sewing on the doll quilts, play boxes, building blocks, puzzles and other quiet games, simple craft work, and of course books to enjoy. For some children who were not particularly interested in acquiring the three R's these other learning situations made the school a pleasant place. They came with eager footsteps and endured the formal lessons as a price to be paid for the privilege of doing the things they wanted to do. And in the whole process they learned a good many of the formal skills, as the record on the achievement tests showed.

The work of the year was centered about the large topics of:

> Foods of Nambé
> Clothing — seasonal
> Pets and their care
> Garden plants
> Insects and animal life of Nambé

The natural science program formed the basis of many of the reading charts. Thus the salamander was in the terrarium because many of our children believed this was a very dangerous animal and had to be shown that it was

harmless and useful. When the frogs in the terrarium disappeared in the fall and were discovered when the children
cleaned the case, the teacher led the discussions which produced this simple chart:

Our Terrarium

Many animals are sleeping in the terrarium.
Two turtles are sleeping in the terrarium.
Two frogs are sleeping in the terrarium.
One salamander is sleeping in the terrarium.
The animals are resting all winter.

The interest in the garden brought forth this discussion,
which is copied from the teacher's diary:

" 'We have some good soil in the little box. I think we
could plant some of the seeds we have brought,' said Pablo.
How deep to plant the seeds, the care of them, and the decision to plant radish seeds afforded opportunities to practice
the use of good English. The children discuss freely the
things they are interested in and thus the planning, discussions, and evaluating periods are considered the most
helpful in the practice of English." The following chart
was developed:

We Plant Seeds

We have good soil in the box.
We will water it well today.
Tomorrow we will plant the seed.
We will cover the seed with the warm soil.
We will water them every day.
When they come up we will watch them grow.
The little radishes will grow under the soil.
When they are big we will eat them.

Much simple reading seatwork was needed. In spite of all the other activities reading was the favorite. Some visitors thought our children had too much seat work. Perhaps so, but it kept several groups busy while the teacher could work with others. There were five levels in the room.

There was no formal writing or arithmetic. It seemed to us that the time could be given more profitably to oral English and reading.

Such a program fits most of the children. By the end of the year the majority are ready to take the next step and pass to the second grade.

SECOND AND THIRD GRADES [7]

"Oh! Miss Jones, he has heem! He has heem! I catch heem but Maclovio he take heem! Will you tell heem to give heem back to me? He is for the story." — The peace of a sunny March morning was shattered. Thirty-four children looked on in consternation and surprise as Perfecto flung himself through the side door of the room and raced toward my desk. Bobbie considerately moved a chair out of his way and I rose to meet him halfway. Finally, we discovered that Perfecto had traded a little wire wagon wheel to Pedro for a spotted salamander. Perfecto put the salamander in a tin can, hid it under a weed on the ditch bank, and went off to play ball. When he returned, can and salamander were gone. He suspected Pedro and righteously accused him, but Pedro told him Maclovio, in the upper

---

[7] Written by Mrs. Ann Jones from her diary and from reports of Mrs. Armijo.

school, had the salamander. Eventually Perfecto was convinced that if Maclovio had the animal he would return it, providing Perfecto hadn't traded it to him in an absentminded moment. Perfecto went to investigate. Maclovio promptly produced the salamander and Perfecto returned triumphant — dangling his social science contribution by the tail. We talked about the salamander, Perfecto told us where he had found him and assured Jennie that he was harmless. We decided to write a story about him after we could learn more about his habits and family, and, until then, placed him in the terrarium. Perfecto supplied him with water and we returned to the daily plans. At it was Monday we had to select a housekeeper for the room, monitors for the playground equipment, a caretaker for the fire, and assistants for the lunch preparations. With social responsibilities assigned and assumed, we sang a few songs and then turned to the morning's work.

Reading, completion, and evaluation of seatwork papers for each group take up the first part of every morning. As individual work is finished each child is free to work at a self-chosen activity until time for him to rejoin his group. The equipment of the schoolroom has been planned around the abilities, interests, and activities of the children. The aquarium contains a small mountain trout and the terrarium, planted with mosses and plants, is placed under the long row of south windows. Low book shelves along the sides of the room hold interesting storybooks and games. There is a library corner with table and chairs, a table for games, and adequate space at the painting easel for two or more children to work at the same time. A play corner shelters the paper dolls and their houses, trucks, balls and bats, and materials and hand looms for weaving. The bulletin boards are low and devoted to interests of the children: nature study, related pictures, bird nests, gourds, odd and colorful rocks. Here there is a place for everything the children contribute or are interested in, and the interests of seven-, eight-, and nine-year-olds are many and varied. The majority of them have learned to read and a whole new world is opened to them. But because they are still very young and must not be confused or discouraged, care must be taken that all experiences are within their understanding and that these understandings permit them to grow socially, emotionally, physically, and academically.

The year's program for this roomful is planned to include familiar experiences which can be developed into new areas as the interests of the children broaden.

The studies are entitled:

Flowers and gardening studied on alternate years.
A study of individuals who made Nambé a more pleasant and better place in which to live.
Bird life and domestic animals studied on alternate years.

A brief description of a typical day shows us at work:

Today, in directed reading, the slowest group read the section "At the Farm," from *At Play,* the middle group read "Blue Barns," from *Round About,* and the best group read "Dick and Tom — Two Ponies," from *We Grow Up.* The slowest and middle groups read orally. The best group was able to read its story silently. Workbooks were occasionally used with the texts but many were too mechanical; consequently, informal seatwork had been prepared for these stories. The children had received a reading foundation in the first grade and during this year words must be added to their vocabulary. They must learn more of the usage of words and tenses in the English language and reading must become daily even more of a tool.

During midmorning recess I played "Squirrels in the Trees" with a small group, refereed a baseball game out of one eye and kept the other on the merry-go-round. During the ball game several of the boys called rules and orders in Spanish. Finally I asked Freddie if they couldn't speak in English. "Of course," grinned Freddie, "we can play just as well in English — but the Spanish always seems to come first." From then on, however, they placed it second for a while.

A few minutes of rest followed the games, some of the children stretched out on the benches — others put their heads on the tables. Then there was time for music and a story. We sang some of the songs about birds and learned a new one about feeding birds. Diana said that soon the birds would be able to find food for themselves because spring was coming.

The reading groups were regrouped for the arithmetic lessons. Group One, composed of the children to whom beginning combinations were being introduced as challenging puzzles, made number cards. The more advanced children in Group Two began an assignment using two-place addition with carrying. Meliton, who knew how to carry, helped Anselmo make his number cards. I worked with individual children at their desks.

While the children were finishing their problems and Group One was participating in a short number drill, Ermelinda and Lola arranged the handwashing paraphernalia and distributed paper towels as the children put their work away and came up to wash. Freddie, Garcedan, and Oracio combed their hair at the mirror, while the rest of the boys combed theirs sight unseen or gave it a lick and a promise. As each child was ready, he took his place at the table where plate, cup, silver, and napkin had been arranged. Lunch was a happy time — we ate slowly and took time to talk. But the children's description fits it better than the narrative:

Lunch Time

Today there was a good lunch. We had macaroni and cheese, vegetable salad, whole wheat biscuits, milk, and apple sauce.

Mrs. Armijo sat at our table. We played a game about our names. Carrie lost her napkin and had to get another. She said, "Mrs. Armijo, will you please excuse me?"

When we finished our lunch Mrs. Armijo said, "You may be excused." Then we went out to play.

At one o'clock the children reassembled in their room for a rest period of thirty minutes, the latter half taken up with storytelling. After resting, pencils were sharpened, paper was distributed, and we started work with spelling and writing. Words from *Stone's List, Most Important 150 Words for Beginning Reading,* and simple, pertinent words from the social science study were used.

Social science work filled the time for the greater part of the afternoon. Plans were made for a bus trip to see a bird feeding board at a neighbor's house. Many birds with which we were familiar were visiting the board, and the children were anxious to watch them. We decided to ask Jennie's father if he would take us on our excursion Wednesday. Then we discussed how we would act while watching the birds. Polly said we would have to be very quiet, and Wilfred added that we would have to be polite to the birds or we would frighten them away. We made a list of the birds we were going to watch for, remembering to notice what they ate, their mannerisms, their colorings, and the way they sang. We talked for a while about the ways in which birds help us, and how we can help the birds by feeding them during the winter and protecting their nests in the summer. Joe said he had seen some of the boys and girls from the upper school tying apples and bread in the trees for the birds to eat in winter. Lily said that her sister in the eighth grade put crumbs outside the classroom window every morning; Vianes added that his brother had built a birdhouse for some birds and put it in a tree by the house.

After the plans were completed the children worked on individual or group activities. Reading for information, discussion, the answering of questions, and the setting up of new questions were among the types of work carried on at different times. Group compositions were written and plans for construction were made, carried out, and evaluated. A few children were ready to do some individual writing and the vocabulary list was the center of attraction.

The making of pencil and crayon illustrations held the attention of others. When the illustrations were finished, stories would be written to explain them. Every day saw new activities started and old ones completed and evaluated. Dramatic plays, songs, and poems related to the study were all enjoyed; an original song or poem might be composed. Special reports might be given, such as the one Perfecto was preparing on the salamander. Here were some of our best opportunities for adding new words to our growing English vocabulary, sharing and putting away tools, being responsible for completing a task, taking turns and sharing responsibilities. The qualities which are essential in every day living are not beyond the capabilities and understandings of second and third graders, if these qualities are an integral part of each day.

A general checking and evaluating period followed the afternoon recess. Anselmo, Bobbie, and Julia needed additional help with their directed reading assignment. Pascualita and Vianes studied spelling words together. A small group got together in one corner of the room and gave each other drill on their number cards. Several children were weaving and sewing. Meliton and Abelito played a game of Chinese checkers. Arabella and Gillie, booklovers, settled at the library table. Dora, Alfredito, and Meliton went to the reading easel and reviewed the group composition, "Our Feeding Board," written the day before. Evelyn sat alone and worked a puzzle; several of the boys gathered about the terrarium, to watch the salamander.

At three o'clock the younger children collected whatever

belongings they wanted to take with them, added a library book to the collection, and wandered off for home. The other children remained to correct an arithmetic assignment prepared during the morning, took part in a snappy drill on addition combinations, and discussed their arithmetic assignment for the next day. New material for the "Reading for Fun" games was introduced. Then we put the room in order, discussed the day's events, and planned the things we wanted to do the next day. Jennie said, as she carefully straightened the bookcases, that she thought we should think of a new name for the salamander. Freddie couldn't find his cap but then finally decided he didn't wear it. Oracio and Wilfred asked if they might play with the ball and bat for a while and offered Candelaria and Stella the doubtful pleasure of being catcher and pitcher.

No one day was ever the same. Sometimes we had birthday parties, frequently one group would invite the others to the auditorium for the dramatization of a story they liked. Another group might want to read a favorite story to the rest of the group. Sometimes we wrote poems, using words the children loved because of their musical sounds or the pictures they presented. Horses plowing the fields, the peacocks walking on the school fence, or the golden glow waving in the wind are examples of the things which were often interpreted in simple rhythm.

The curriculum was based upon the academic needs of the children and community resources. A profusion of fall flowers in the valley naturally led us into the study of flowers and plants in September. At least once during each

PLATE I

The school bell is not only a symbol of opportunity for the children, but also in a community school it rings for everyone

Photo Courtesy Soil Conservation Service

PLATE II

The grounds of the school provide space for a
fascinating outdoor laboratory

study, a walk was taken around the village to see all the flower gardens. This provided excellent opportunities in development of keen observation and promoted conversation in English.

In a few instances, as a result of the study and the contacts made during the study walks, more thought was given to the spring planning of the gardens. For instance, height of flowers, time of blooming, and pleasing combinations were considered. Those plants which hold the soil and which do not require too much water were sometimes included for the first time. Flowers that depleted the soil, did not hold the soil, or used a great deal of water were sometimes omitted from the gardens. Where water was a real problem and the economic status of the family low, a few flower gardens were turned into vegetable gardens.

The introduction of tulips, jonquils, and daffodils into the school garden led to their use in the community. Narcissus had never been used in the homes until they were grown in a pottery bowl on the library table at school.

Compositions, of which the following is an example, were developed:

The Cosmos

We dug a cosmos plant from the school garden. The plant has a big stalk. Many branches grow on the stalk. The branches have many thin leaves. The leaves look like grama grass. Each big leaf has many little leaves. The big leaves are opposite on the branches.

The flowers are at the top of the branches. All cosmos have eight petals. Usually cosmos are pink, white, or red. There are buds at the top of the branches, too. Buds grow into flowers.

Some of the flowers bloom quicker than the others. The center of the flower has the seeds. It is yellow. The seeds are black and long.

The roots are very interesting. The tap root has many little roots growing on it. It brings food and water from the soil for the plant. The side roots are to hold the plant in the soil. They get food for the plant. They hold the good soil so that the water cannot wash it away. If the plant did not have roots it could not live.

We have many cosmos in our garden. Cosmos plants are good for us to grow because they hold the soil and do not need much water.

The middle and weakest group would combine and compose a story simple enough for all to read, as:

The Cosmos

> The cosmos plant is tall.
> It has many green leaves.
> It has pretty red flowers.
> The flowers have little, black seeds.
> The plant has a long root.
> There are many little roots on the long root.
> Many of us have cosmos in our gardens.

One study was culminated with a flower show at the school community fair. The children competed for first, second, and third prize ribbons. Flower experts from outside the valley were invited to be judges and award the prizes.

The second unit of study was Community Helpers. There was a constant effort on the part of the staff to dignify all honest labor. It was thought that an area of interest which provided an opportunity to study the occupation of the adults of the community would be helpful. But the study actually grew from the interests of the children themselves. One morning, in circle discussion, Ernesto said, "Pedro's mother is helping my mother put the mud on the house." Fabiola added that Carrie's grandmother was helping. The other children described the recent plastering of their houses and we decided to take a walk to Ernesto's house to watch the plastering. None of the women working on the house spoke English but Ernesto was an able interpreter. His mother invited the teacher to plaster, so she took off her coat and "threw some mud" amid laughter from the women and children. The group composition developed by the A reading group follows:

Plastering Ernesto's House

There were four women plastering Ernesto's house. They threw the mud on the wall of the house. The mud stuck to the wall. The women smoothed the mud. They smoothed it with their hands and with trowels.

Carrie's grandmother was on the roof of the house. We saw Pedro's mother giving mud to her. We saw Ernesto's brother bringing mud in a tub. The tub was on a sled. A horse pulled the sled.

Ernesto and Abelito mixed some mud. First they dug some dirt from the hole with a shovel. Ernesto's brother put some water on the dirt. He got the water from the ditch. Ernesto put some straw in the mud. Me mixed it with the hoe. When it was well mixed it was ready to be put on the house.

When the desire to learn more about the school nurse arose, a committee was selected to interview Miss Casias and invite her to come and talk to us. The following chart tells the story of her work:

The School Nurse

Miss Casias is our nurse. She tries to keep the people well. She vaccinated the babies so that they will not have diphtheria, smallpox, and typhoid fever.

Miss Casias goes to our houses. She tells our mothers how to keep the babies well. She tells them what kind of food to give the babies. She tells them to put the food where the flies will not get on it. She tells them to put netting over the babies to keep off the flies.

Miss Casias tells our mothers to take the babies to see the doctor every month. Our mothers take the babies to the clinic to see the doctor. The clinic is in the school.

Miss Casias tells our fathers where to put the toilets and the wells. She tells them to put screens on the wells, so that the flies cannot get in. She tells them not to put the wells near the toilets.

Some of the other helpers studied were: the farmer, the ditch rider, the school carpenter, the priest, the mailman, the school bus driver, the teachers, the doctor, and other community friends and neighbors.

The work in natural science seemed as significant as anything done. Peculiar superstitions had clouded many things in nature for these people and the school attempted to lighten them through education. One day Gilberto said, "Which book has some stories about toads? My father wants to know if they eat the lettuce." Some of the people in the community began to realize that use could be made of the resources offered in the classrooms.

The school also made more and more use of community
resources. Early one spring morning, a swarm of bees settled in a tree in front of the school. The children watched
two of the parents hive them and, as they were interested,
we took time to talk and read about bees.

Thus, through observation, reading, discussion, and consideration of each other's opinions, a valuable beginning
was given these children in the problems of living, and a
foundation in the problems of learning.

<h2 style="text-align:center">FOURTH AND FIFTH GRADES [8]</h2>

A Study of Irrigation, Water, the Land, and Man

From eight o'clock in the morning until four-thirty in
the afternoon the fourth and fifth grade room was full of
children and of evidences of their interests and activities.
The room was sunny, with large white-curtained windows
and equipment similar to that of the other classrooms.

The forty-two children in the room were grouped into
four flexible groups according to abilities and chronological
ages. One group consisted of nine boys who were retarded
readers and had been "socially promoted" because of age
and interests. The other three groups were formed according to reading abilities and background. However, the fact
that a child was in the B reading group did not necessarily
mean that all of his activities were confined to that group.
In this room, as in the others, each child took part in the
group which would benefit him most and in which he could
contribute to the best of his ability. Gilbert, for instance,

---

[8] Written by Margaret Wyss from her diary.

was in the A reading and social science groups, in the C spelling group and the B arithmetic group. Mike was in the B reading group, but he often took part in the discussions of the A group because he was interested in the work they were doing and because he was a good thinker and often needed more stimulation than he received in the B group. Gloria and Diana took part in the discussions of the A group and in the arithmetic work. They worked independently in writing and spelling, in social science, and on arithmetic assignments because they were much more advanced than the rest of the group and capable of doing more difficult work. The nine boys worked entirely by themselves, but shared the experiences of the group in planning, in story-telling, and in the general room activities. In addition to the academic program, wood working and work with the soil were stressed. With the exception of the nine boys the reading ability of the group was average. There were seven children whose reading ability was above average for the grade and their work was planned to meet their needs and stimulate their interests.

This is a partial report of the work done by the fourth and fifth grades during a school year. It does not include all of the program nor constitute a complete report of the year's work. There is little mention of the time given the skill subjects, but all materials were organized and read in directed reading periods. Spelling, arithmetic, and language were an integral part of each day's work. The most significant fact about the study is that it continued for the entire year, broadening as the interests of the children broadened and developing as their understanding developed.

When we planned the work for these grades we realized that the studies must contribute to the daily life of the children and also lead them out to other parts of the unknown world. Their interest in other peoples and other lands was of great importance, but until they had found a common denominator, for their own use, of the needs and interrelationship of people, it was useless for them to risk becoming lost in other lands of seemingly unrelated customs and people. The curriculum chosen must give them some means of exploring other environments and communities through the understanding, not only of their own community, but of the basic needs of people everywhere. Such an approach to the studies was found through the land and the land's primary need in this country — water. General plans for the study were drawn up in the following outline:

The Study of Irrigation, Water, the Land, and Man

I. The Water Cycle
   A. Behavior of water
      1. Movement of water in and from the earth
         a. Evaporation, transpiration, absorption
            i. e. rivers, lakes, ponds, wells, etc.
         b. Storage of water on earth
      2. Water pumps on the earth
         a. Plants, trees, flowers, etc.
      3. The story of rain, snow, sleet, and hail
      4. Fog and mist in the water cycle
      5. Cloud formations and movements in relation to the water cycle.

II. Sources of Nambé's water supply

    A. Rainfall and snow water from the mountains
        1. Nambé River
            a. Source of river
            (1) Forest (ground litter, humus, root zones)

III. Uses of water in Nambé

    A. Irrigation
        1. System of irrigation
            a. Use of river and ditches
            (1) Cleaning, etc.
    B. Drinking water — water for household use
        1. Wells
            a. Sanitation
    C. Power
        1. Electricity
    D. Use of water by plants and animals

IV. Conservation of water in Nambé

    A. Methods of conservation used
        1. School ground
        2. Community, i. e., plants, trees, contours, dams, reservoirs, wells, storage tanks

V. Interdependence of water, the land and man, plants and animals

    A. Ways in which man uses water
        1. Irrigation
        2. Stock
        3. Drinking and household uses
    B. Uses of water by soil, plants and animals

VI. Importance of water to all people, plants and animals

 A. Following of water routes
  1. Nambé River
  2. Rio Grande

 B. Uses of rivers and dams
  1. Mills
  2. Power
  3. Electricity

 C. Different sources and means of obtaining water
  1. Source of city water in comparison with source of country water supply, i. e., water systems, reservoirs, etc.

VII. Water, soil, and man

 A. The world we live in
  1. Interdependence of all people
  2. Balance of nature and man's use of resources

 B. Water and the Southwest
  1. Early history of the territory
   a. Early methods of irrigation and farming
  2. New Mexico today
   a. Source of water supply
   b. Uses of water
   c. Supply of water
   d. Man's need of water

There is not space to tell of all the experiences, trips, and activities connected with this big subject of water, but two written accounts speak for themselves.

Water

The water in the terraces waited in little pools until it went into the soil. It did not run down to the playground.

The plants held the water and the soil. The way the terraces are built helped to hold the water.

Sometimes some of the water in the terraces evaporates before it goes into the soil.

We did not lose much in the school grounds. Some of the water went into the roots of the trees. Some of the water went into the roots of the plants.

The water that evaporated was not wasted because it goes into the air and comes back to the earth.

It rained because the air could not hold all the water.

Where the Water in Nambé Comes From

We get our water in Nambé from many places. Some of our water comes from wells. Some of the people get their water from ponds. Freddie's father uses water from a pond for irrigation. Lorencito's father does too.

Water from the river is carried to the farms by irrigation ditches. There are many of these ditches in Nambé.

The different ditches have different names. One of the ditches is called the Cano Ditch. About thirty men use the water from this ditch for irrigation. There are eight more ditches in the village. These ditches are the Nuevo Ditch, the Chano, the Mocho, and the Rincon. The men use these ditches to carry the water for irrigation.

Sometimes when the river has too much water, the men take some water out and put it in the ditches. This keeps the river from flooding. If the river flooded it would go over its banks and destroy the crops and wash the soil away. If we do not help to keep the water where it belongs, water does not always help us.

If there is not a pond at the end of the ditch the water goes into the arroyo. Sometimes the water from the river goes into the arroyo. Many times the arroyo takes the water back to the Nambé River. The water from the river that is not used for irrigation goes into the Rio Grande. The Rio Grande goes into the Gulf of Mexico.

We use the water from the river for irrigation. We get our drinking water from wells and springs and ponds. The water from these is much cleaner and purer than river water.

The study of water broadened until it became more than a social science unit to be explored at certain times during the day, but a means of understanding the world. The children began to realize that they had a place in the general scheme of things. The work their fathers did and the work they did on their fathers' farms, was all part of a great country of people working together.

Then one December morning Wilfred came in and said, "We are fighting in the war!" and so began a study of Europe. This sudden departure to Europe had not been planned. As can be seen by the outline, we meant to follow the rivers of Nambé to other parts of the United States. We were forced to go to Europe because the children were interested, but they had no conception of Europe other than the one presented by maps and textbooks. We had first explored our community, and it was the basic understanding which developed from that study which enabled the children to understand the people of Europe. Always they compared other countries with their own land and noted the factors which caused the differences. They had learned some of the simple facts upon which living is dependent:

that men and plants and animals must have water to live; that soil must be saved because all things come from the land; that men must work together; that countries must have communication and means of transportation; and that men must work to maintain a balance between their needs and the natural resources they use. The children had always known that there were other people in the world but they had never given these people much thought. Now they found these people had the same needs they had. They had to have land for crops, clothes to wear, and houses to live in. But this knowledge did not come in one year. These children were in the prefirst room when the project started and had the benefit of several years of planned curricula and skillful teaching. This study was developed with them during the last year of the project. Our work in the social studies integrated the experiences and interests of the year, but the success of the study was facilitated because these children were increasingly capable of using the skills of reading, writing, and arithmetic as tools of learning.

A Day in the Sixth and Seventh Grades [9]

The sixth and seventh grade room has an air of being lived in. The large windows on the east side hold a profusion of plants — geraniums, begonias, cactus, and many others. In the early morning the sunlight makes the whole room bright; in the later afternoon it softens the outlines of the old-fashioned scarred desks and reflects from the water in the aquarium and the bright pictures on the wall.

---

[9] Written from the diary of Mrs. Victoria de Sanchez.

Under the windows three bookcases are full of reading material and brief lists indicate the contents of each shelf of books. Another case holds the games the boys have made for classroom use, and on the wall is the checking list for games which are taken home overnight. In the wall of the southeast corner is the niche which the children built to hold their collection of rocks, carvings, and material received from an Australian school with which they corresponded. In the northeast corner of the room is a tall cupboard which holds books, chalk, crayons, carving tools, wood for the craftwork, scissors, patterns for sewing, sewing boxes, and alabastine paint for the murals. One side of the cupboard is used as a correspondence bulletin board, and letters have been postmarked from Georgia, Alaska, Washington, D. C., Canada, and Australia. In the back of the room are two sewing machines, the aquarium, and the teacher's desk. In the corner is the bookcase which the boys built for the library books. The blackboard in the back of the room has been covered with brown wrapping paper to be used as bulletin boards. When a mural is being painted it is usually spread across this space so the children will have enough room. At present, pictures of New Mexico song and game birds have been collected and placed here by the children. The east end is covered by a large map of the world with countries and cities of current interest outlined in blue and red crayon. Above the board is a mounted collection of bird nests with explanatory stories which have been written by the children.

The blackboard on the west wall is used for assignments

and for individual practice in arithmetic and handwriting by the children. Above the board Leopoldo and Merced hung the bird stories which were written by the different groups last week. There is a small bulletin board on the same wall on which we have placed pictures pertaining to irrigation and soil conservation. These pictures were used to initiate the new unit, "Irrigation in Nambé, New Mexico, and the Southwest." They are of immediate interest at present, as the men and boys are digging out and cleaning the irrigation ditches in preparation for the spring irrigation. Another bulletin board has a caption "Good Work" and the best written work is posted here each week. At present it has also a picture of a sulphur mine which Soilo found in *Life Magazine* and posted after a group discussion about minerals and different soils.

As one corner of the west wall juts out, we are given ample wall space for a natural science display board, which at present has samples of soils in glass tubes with captions and two small hornets' nests brought by Miguela, who has eyed them apprehensively ever since Oracio told her they might possibly contain sleeping hornets.

Above the blackboard on the south wall the children painted several bird pictures. The boys also drew pictures of game birds on the wall space under the board — realistic road runners gravely confronting one another and a pheasant that seems to prance toward the corner. Under the edge of the board, and easily accessible to all members of the group, is a rack holding varied materials, such as 4H Club material, games, songs, arithmetic drill cards, road maps, penmanship booklets, and indirectly supervised exercises in arithmetic and language.

In the center of the room are desks for thirty-one children. In the front of the room there are chairs and a table for the work or discussion circle. There is space in the room for the children to work on their individual projects of carving, drawing, writing, sewing, and reading. The desks can be moved when more space is needed for groups to work together. Usually by three o'clock in the afternoon the sixth graders overflow into the hall, the storeroom, and the school grounds for work upon different projects.

This morning Merced was sitting comfortably on the floor at the end of the hall; he was against the wall, idly strumming his guitar, while Frank attempted to aid Roy in the intricacies of multiplication. Emily kept a watchful eye on the fourth and fifth grade room, where her small brother was gleefully fishing for the goldfish in the aquarium. As soon as the room was opened (the janitor always locks it and wanders off) a group gathered around the radio to listen to music. Some of the children looked at magazines, Tony picked up his carving, and Abelino and Roy, having given up the arithmetic, came in after the ball and bat. Leopoldo departed with the basketball, and Emily, seeing that her young charge had left the fish for the swings, started a checker game with Laura.

Horacio and Viola offered to remove the social studies reading material from the bookcases and replace it with material on irrigation. While they took the used books to the storeroom Elisaida went into the seventh and eighth grade room to borrow ten copies of "How and Why Experiments" to be used in the study of irrigation. Manuel enlisted the aid of Merced in putting all the carving and carpentry tools away in the library and in sweeping the floor in preparation for the weekly music session held with a WPA music teacher. Mary added water to the aquarium, fed the fish and watered the plants in the window, and then came up to the teacher and whispered that Rosalie had brought her new dress to show her, but was too shy to tell her about it. While a group of us were admiring the dress, neatly packed in tissue paper, Manuel came in and remarked, with a disgusted look in the direction of the dress, that it was nine o'clock. He went out to ring the bell, and children from the grounds poured into the hall, extracted themselves from the main current, and went into their respective rooms.

During discussion of current events and the morning newscast, Jose noticed the sun shining in the eyes of several students, so he drew the shades. After the daily plans were completed, Nestor noticed how dark it had become, so he put the shades up again. Nestor looked around in annoyance, and Emily, with a look of scorn for boys in general, lowered them from the top.

The first part of every morning is given to social science work and projects. This morning the study lesson for the A group was entitled "Use — Don't Waste," a lesson on the use of forest lands and trees. Several questions were given

PLATE III

The fathers come to observe what the boys are
learning but end by taking part in the work

Photo Courtesy Soil Conservation Service

PLATE IV

These pupils are learning lessons from the natural
resources of the community

the children to be answered in the discussion period. The questions were based upon a reading assignment which had been made for this morning:

1. With what was the forest floor covered? Describe what is under the first layer of leaves.
2. What is the name of this black soil and tell why it is better than the soil on the playground.
3. Give four ways in which the humus in our forests helps the trees and the rivers.
4. Does the floor of the forest in the Nambé mountains help the people in the valley? Explain your answer.
5. What problems do burned forests bring to people?

These questions were given to provoke critical thinking, purposeful oral English discussion, and bring out the relationship between the use of natural resources and human activities.

The assignment for group B was the study of four pictures on land use with the following caption under them: "In each of these pictures notice what is being done to heal the gullies and save the soil. How many of these methods have we used in our community and on our school grounds?"

After studying these pictures, the children were to write paragraphs answering the questions in the captions. A vocabulary list, which had been compiled by the group during the week, was placed where the children could see it and make use of it in the proper spelling of words that they used in their paragraphs. The list is used for reference and words used in the spelling lessons are taken from it.

Word List

destroy	owner	transplant	across
form	frightened	alone	easily
picture	Indian	washed	grown
arroyo	terraces	shrubs	turn
since	roads	receive	own
watch	protected	third	cover
places	enough	first	rock

As the groups settled down to work, Group C took their places in the discussion circle and read orally the three short pages of "Kinds of Soil" in *Pathways in Science — Out of Doors.* After discussing the story and information gathered from the reading of other material, they composed a group story.

How Important Is Soil?

Soil is one of the most important natural resources on which people depend for a living. The best soil contains humus, dead plant and animal matter. It also contains bacteria which help keep it rich. Soil is so important that people cannot live without it. People grow gardens, orchards, and many other farm crops on the soil. From the soil man feeds his family and his farm animals. He also raises food for people who live in communities around him. Cities depend on the soil for their supply of food. The man who works the soil raises food for the cities. If a man does not have soil, he cannot raise plants. He cannot have grass and forests. Without plants and animals man cannot live because he depends on these for food.

After the story had been completed and we were discussing how humus forms, Jose said he would like to go outside and bring a piece of wood that showed how ants keep "grinding" the wood so it goes into the ground and helps to make humus. He went out and returned with a piece of an old tree trunk which had a layer of fine sawdust on one side. We discussed the slow disintegration of the wood and the difference in soil in the forest and on the mesa. Jose said the mesa soil was hard and "no good" because there was no humus from decayed plants in the soil and no plants to hold the moisture.

Valentin, who reads poorly, but can make anything grow, suggested that the group write a story on "How Soil Is Made." Manuel said he didn't think the book we were reading had anything about that subject. The children looked through the table of contents and found a short chapter on the material they wanted. It was decided that the group would read these pages on the following day and then compose another story. Oracio said one of the new library books had a story about soil in it. We asked him to read it and tell us about it the following day.

This group of children is unable to write long individual stories for it is difficult for them to put their thoughts on paper. There is a definite need for greater proficiency in the English language, and to meet this need group discussion is encouraged and group compositions are put on permanent tagboard charts and used both for reference and reading lessons. This morning the children were given mimeographed seatwork pertaining to the circle discussion, consisting of questions to be answered in one sentence or short paragraphs.

The work assigned to groups A and B took a large

amount of time, as the children had to look up the answers to their questions in the social science reading material, think them through, and write them in their own words. After the C group went to their seats the work of the children was supervised and checked for language and punctuation. Some of the group had finished and were working on arithmetic, spelling, or language exercises. Others, who worked more slowly, needed assistance in composing their sentences or organizing their material. The papers of a few, who had finished in record time, were checked and the children who had not worked carefully settled down to do a more thorough job. Abelino finished his paper, quietly asked to have it checked, and once more helped Roy tackle the arithmetic.

At ten-thirty Nestor remarked that it was time for recess and held up his paper for a last minute checking. The boys told the girls they would play them a game of baseball and the girls accepted the invitation provided the boys would lend them two players as they were short on fielders. Lorenzo, the recreational director, acted as umpire. The teacher played volley ball with a group of girls who scorned baseball.

After recess the children formed a line at the drinking fountain and then resumed their various tasks. Benancio and Horacio (retarded readers) had finished their individual work and gone with Lorenzo to help him set out iris plants. Every day certain individuals or groups work on the school grounds to learn correct land practices, to apply practices discussed in the classroom, to develop pride in right practices, and to learn to use their hands as well as their minds.

Group A discussed the lesson on the correct usage of the forest. The seatwork was assigned and each child given ample time to think out and explain his answer. The discussion covered the relationship between forests, other natural resources, and man. Abelino summed up the whole discussion when he said, "We can see how everything works together. The flood at Española was caused because there was so much rain and snow in the mountains and the land and river couldn't hold all the water. Too many trees have been destroyed in the mountains and this hurts our land."

We discussed the uses of natural resources, and the assignment for the next day was "The Uses of the Forest to Man and Animals and the Enemies of the Forest." The purpose of this lesson was to teach man's dependence on forests and the fact that man has been and still is the forest's worst enemy. Through realization of the importance of the forests and of man's responsibility in caring for them, the children have opportunity to learn that prevention is one of the most important steps in successful planning and use of natural resources.

Group A went to their seats to read the assigned material for the following day and Group B came to the circle to read the stories they wrote about the pictures. Santiago dropped into his place in the circle and announced proudly, "I had an awful time with this!" Remembering the days when Santiago refused to be interested in anything but races and playing hookey, the teacher thankfully asked him to read his story first. He beamed and proceeded:

Once there were roads here. When new roads were made the old one was left alone. When it rained the water ran fast and took the soil with it because there were no plants to hold it. Then the roads became gullies. At last, to save the soil, men made check dams. The dams caught the soil and water that ran down the road every time it rained. Then grass began to grow. The grass roots will hold the soil and soon all the soil will be saved.

There was little discussion of Santiago's paper. The children approved it and turned to Nestor for his contribution:

The Indian in the picture is terracing his land so that he can save it. He had made the terraces so that the wind and rain cannot destroy his land. He planted grass on the terraces to hold the soil.

Elisaida said that the terraces in the picture were built unlike the ones on the school ground; the terraces in the picture were across the length of a field while ours were square and built more "like squares." "Yes," answered Manuel, "but we have long ones too. There are two between here and the lower building; you look for them at noon."

The stories which the children read were evaluated and discussed by the group. The oral discussion provided opportunity for experience in English and gave an excellent chance to stress correct usage of word forms.

B group, still continuing their discussion, gathered up their papers, collected the arithmetic problems they were to work on, and went to their seats. Some members of Group A, having finished their assignments, were working on arithmetic drills and others were working on individual projects. Group C were working on reading seatwork which was checked individually. The children had read a story, "Protected Wild Life," silently, and they were ready for the comprehension test, consisting of multiple questions asking content, identification of characters, and the reason for certain important actions which took place in the story. After the test the children came to the circle and the papers were checked and mistakes and ideas in the story which had not been understood were discussed. The next day's assignment was Part II of the story, or had been until the circle informed the teacher that they had read this part too. Virginia said they could answer the questions given in the mimeographed seatwork and Manuel asked if he could write a story about the wild animals he had seen. We all agreed that individual stories would be fun to do, and added them to the assignment. There was time between groups to check the arithmetic drills orally and to discuss the reading for skill seatwork.

Group A came to the circle for the last period before lunch. Tommy passed the books and, after Dora read us a poem she thought the group would enjoy, the children read aloud, stopping often to discuss or comment. This group is able to move much more swiftly than the others, as they have a better command of English and their reading is for pleasure and information with very little remedial work. As a group they are very interested and usually supplement the stories read with other related materials which they find. While the A group finished reading, Jose, who has no confidence in the way we watch time, brought a pail of water, arranged the basin and paper towels, hunted up the soap which Dora had tucked out of sight when she had put the room in order yesterday, and the children washed their hands while the group in the circle finished reading. At twelve o'clock we went down to the lower building for lunch, Manuel carefully pointing out the long terraces to Elisaida on the way down.

The afternoon session began at one o'clock. The teacher read a chapter of *Tom Sawyer* during the rest period. Two reading groups of twenty minutes each were held for Groups C and B respectively. Group C read for comprehension and Group B read for comprehension and speed. Group A worked on multiplication and division by one and two numbers. The most advanced children worked on addition and subtraction of fractions. The papers were brought to the circle to be checked and individual children worked problems on the board. After mistakes in accuracy had been checked, the children played an arithmetic game with oral thought problems. They were then given individual work dealing with their specific difficulties. Groups B and C came back to the circle for checking and work on addition, subtraction, and multiplication. This was followed by a timed check-test.

At two-fifteen the blackboard space was crowded with children working out problems. The desks had been arranged so groups could share drill cards and work together in competitive arithmetic games. Abelino had gotten Roy started on a set of problems and was helping Mary, whose logic stopped at problems and whom a column of numbers terrified. Group C came to the circle for the checking of their arithmetic papers and for individual and group work at the blackboard. The children who received perfect scores on their papers returned to their seats to copy the letters they had written and corrected the previous day. The rest of the group spent more time in board work and were given practice problems to work at their desks. The same procedure was followed with the B group, with a difference in the level of work. When the work with this group was finished the teacher worked with individuals, explaining steps, checking papers, assigning drills, and watching to see that work was neatly done, that problems were thought through, and that each child understood what he was doing and why he was doing it. José again informed us that it was time for recess, and the boys deserted the baseball game for basketball with Lorenzo and the eighth graders. The girls carried on by themselves, and, while they weren't as strict about rules as the boys usually were, they managed to play a better game than in the morning.

After recess Groups A and B had spelling. The list was made up of common words misspelled in letters, composi tions, and individual stories. The papers were checked with each child individually so he could see his spelling and penmanship errors. The pupils who had misspelled the words studied them again. Spelling for the C group followed the same procedure except that this list of words was shorter, less difficult, and more time was given to the use of words in oral sentences to broaden understanding.

By three-fifteen the last spelling group was over and we were all ready to participate in the last period of the day. This period is flexible. The children are allowed to pursue free activities related to their social studies, do research for special problems, 4H Club work, or to do additional work on individual reading, arithmetic, spelling, and writing. The different activities are of wide enough range to take care of children of both low and high academic standing. The activities allow them to use their hands to develop creativeness, resourcefulness, responsibility, and self-reliance. It is during this period, more than at any other time of the day, that we come together with time to share problems, discuss plans, and evaluate the work that is being done. The period is really the culmination of the day's work and the room becomes even more of a work shop. Today José went to the wood workshop to work on a toy rabbit; Valentin worked in the hall on a reed table he was making for his mother; Luisa, Miquela, and Mary worked in the back room on the dresses they are making; Merced and Santiago illustrated some charts. In one corner of the room Ray and Tomas were working together on a letter to the Commissioner of Education in Alaska for information on whether Eskimos lived in igloos or not. In yesterday's reading lesson there were conflicting sources of information and opinion and the boys were elected to write a letter to settle the question. In another corner Dora was helping Jose with the difficult words in the story of conversation. Members of the C group were working on book ends for their homes and six of the girls had gone to the cooking class, delighted with the prospect of making tapioca pudding. The practical training they receive in reading recipes, measuring ingredients, cooking, and planning meals is invaluable. The academic standing of the girls in today's class is low, and they will profit more by learning to be better housewives than by struggling with division and multiplication. Elisaida, who was cutting out a pair of pajamas, asked after the girls left if the ingredients for tapioca pudding could be found in Nambé, as she wished to make some for her mother.

At four-five we suddenly realized how late it was. Nestor collected the carving tools and put them away. The children put the supplies they had been using back into the cupboard. Tony collected the language papers and placed them in the envelope by the worktable so they could be checked in the morning, and Horacio and Mary straightened the library shelves. Dora came in with paint on her nose from the mural on which she had been working and asked is she might take the checkers home for the night. Rosabelle asked for help on the dress she was making for her baby sister and said she would wait after school. By four-thirty the room was empty, except for Merced's guitar and José's cap — both eloquent reminders of the owners, who could be seen playing basketball on the court outside. The teacher closed the door on the used-up day, watched the game for a few minutes, and then walked on down the road to see why Ben had not been in school and inquire about Frances' mumps. As Tommy went whizzing by on his bicycle, asking impishly if she would like to ride, she reflected that one of the nicest things about a teaching day is that it is never ended — life with the children is just transferred to different surroundings.

(Editor's note: The large topics for the year's work in these grades are: The Study of Records, Animals, and Plants on the Earth; Man and the World He Lives In.)

A DAY IN THE UPPER GRADES ROOM [10]

As I left the house this morning, Roberto and Mike were going by and I walked along with them. It was 8:15 when we got to school. Several children were already there, and as I opened the door of the room they rushed in to get balls and bats. Some of the children listened to the newscast, to be able to contribute something during our discussion of current events. The children are vitally interested in the developments of the war, for during the first part of the year they learned much about the present war. This interest has been kept up by reading newspapers, magazines, as well as through discussions and listening to the radio. Another group of children took the Chinese checkers and gathered around one of the small tables to play a game; several went to their desks to practice multiplication tables with which they had been having trouble; some went to work on some summaries of a current study on conservation; some had carving to do; some played blackboard games; some gathered in small groups to talk; others had

---

[10] Written by Frank Angel from his diary, reports, and notes.

brought their guitars and were strumming them and practicing new strokes, for it was the day for the WPA music
teacher to come. Reuben and Betty were discussing a copy
of a mural by Diego Rivera, which was posted on the bulletin board in the hall. Antonia and Manuel started a
basketball game. Irene helped me put up some conservation pictures and captions, which the children had written,
stimulated by some pictures which they had secured on loan
by writing to the regional office of the Soil Conservation
Service.

Picture of Contour Furrows on Range Land

Contour furrows help to hold water so it will infiltrate into
the ground. We need to practice contouring in Nambé. —
Emma, 7th grade.

Picture of Men Making Terraces

The soil is being protected by building small dams and terraces. Grass is planted to help control runoff water. — Pita,
7th grade.

Our room is arranged so that there are four rows of mov-
able desks placed close together, leaving space for a circle
of chairs, in which groups can come together for planning,
discussion, or reading without disturbing people who are
working at their seats. We also have three small tables
which we use for display of work or other needs. In one
corner we have a supply cupboard. There are also three
bookcases in the room, one reserved for reference materials
— encyclopedias and dictionaries; the other two for readers,
arithmetics, library books, and social science materials. We

have three large outline maps made by the children: one of New Mexico, another of the United States, and another of Europe. The boys and girls had felt the lack of a map on which to show the German conquests in Europe and mark the changes taking place, so they made the outline map of Europe, and when it proved a success, the other two were suggested. Many of the geographical concepts and historical movements have been traced on these maps; and as these maps are washable, it is easy to keep them clean. In addition we had a set of commercial maps.

When the bell rang, at nine, the children came in. A line formed at the fountain and as each new arrival came, he took his place in line. Luis came in pushing and jostling others to get in front, and was promptly ousted by Irene and Odulia with the admonishment, "Don't be so rude, Luis, can't you wait for your turn?" He wanted to argue, but I interfered and asked him if he didn't think Irene was right.

When I came into the room several had gotten out their materials and were beginning to work. I noticed Pedro going over to a corner to see whether the willow table he had made from native willows and orange crates was dry. Abelino sat at the wall niche, comparing his carving with some of the completed pieces. As I came in he showed me his carved goose, saying, "Look, I even got the 'crop' on right." When all were settled, I asked if there were any news to bring up. Pedro told us about a death with which we were all concerned. A young man from the community had died in an accident in Arizona and his body had been brought home. Pedro said the accident was caused because the driver had been going too fast and was drunk. We discussed the matter of excess speed and intoxication while driving.

Antonio volunteered that he had read in the Santa Fe *New Mexican* that the Croats and Serbs had united in Yugoslavia to fight against possible German aggression. We located Yugoslavia on our outline map. A discussion followed on the possibility of conquest of the Balkan Peninsula. Basilia said she didn't know it was called the Balkan Peninsula. The present war has given us many opportunities to learn about countries of the world. A common misconception we have encountered is: the children thought Europe and Africa were countries or sometimes continents, using these interchangeably. The use of maps has corrected this.

Ted, our only Anglo, remarked that the newspapers were full of news about strikes at the Ford plant. We got into a discussion of labor rights, unions, agitators, and workers. Adela thought the laborers were right, because she could see why they should have a share of the profits during the war boom. Soilo thought labor was taking advantage of the situation. Ernestine thought the President ought to call out the army and make the strikers work. We all agreed the country needs armaments to help Britain. I suggested that a weakness of democracy was that when individuals were given responsibilities and didn't meet them adequately, everyone suffered. Reuben said, "Yes, like Librado yesterday, when he took advantage of the freedom in the room." During our first study on the present war, the children had learned much about other forms of government in the world. They had been much concerned with the preservation of democracy and had made a list of the ways in which they, in their daily lives, could live more democratically. They had read several books on democracy and were still very much interested.

Our next plans were about our social science study in conservation. The class is divided into groups, based upon reading abilities. The C group is seeking information about plants and animals. This study had its beginning during a discussion period, when the ways in which the community could be improved had been brought up. Since Nambé is a farming community, and the people are dependent upon the soil for their living, there was an excellent purpose in studying methods of land use.

The B group was working on related seatwork for the chapter, "The Destruction of the Grasslands" in Bruner-Smith *Social Studies,* Book III. This group had made a bibliography of materials which could be used in answering questions. It had written to experts in the Soil Conservation Service, the Forest Service, and the State Agricultural College, asking for information and free materials. It had asked the Soil Conservation Service to send a man to talk to us on land use. The experience has been very valuable. The A group did most of its own research. It had finished reading and collecting information from various publications. After a group discussion, it had agreed to reorganize all the information it had gotten on land use, in order to

PLATE V

An expert from the Soil Conservation Service teaches
the older boys how to heal an arroyo

Photo Courtesy Soil Conservation Service

PLATE VI

In a dry land every drop of moisture is valuable

Photo Courtesy Soil Conservation Service

present it to the fifth and sixth grades, who were studying about irrigation and had asked for the material.

Today I had a rather large group in the circle who were having trouble with oral reading. In order to give them help in attacking words and in pronunciation, we were using *Improving Your Reading* which has an excellent section on word difficulties. The exercises consist of word lists with similar sounds and comprehension checks. As the children were called upon to read these lists they encountered words that they would not attack and would look to me for help. Instead of pronouncing the word I pointed out to them similarities between words they knew and got them to use these as clues in attacking new words.

We had planned to work on our social science unit next. The study we were working on was "How Nature Maintains Her Balance," a soil conservation unit. This was initiated because of the interest shown by the children in problems related to land use in the community. Previous units on food, clothing, transportation, have all been related and traced to the soil. The land around the community is badly eroded and in many instances abused, with the result that the standards of living are lower than they would have been if the land had been cared for properly. Keeping these facts in mind, the children had formulated questions which they wished to investigate and find data on. Some of these were:

How are standards of living related to the land?
Why is the land around Nambé so eroded?
What can be done to prevent erosion and correct it?

Do plants and animals have anything to do with erosion?
What are good crops for Nambé farmers to plant?

These questions had been written on tagboard and placed on the wall for reference. As printed material to answer their questions is scarce and often not available at the children's level, they had planned to find material relating to their problem by other means, such as writing to Soil Conservation Service, the county agent, asking older residents in the community, going on excursions into the community to observe erosion and land practices, and asking conservation experts to give talks on proper land use. The children had secured abundant material from these sources. One group of pupils had read several bulletins and were writing up their findings.

After our social science we worked on reading. All the children need directed reading and provision was made for it. The A and B groups worked in the room; the C group, needing more remedial attention, went to the principal every day. The other groups worked on arithmetic and language.

After plans were made the C group came to the circle for directed work. We read a chapter on "Herbs, Shrubs, Trees, Flowers" in the book *Pathways in Science*. We kept in mind one of the questions which had been asked at the beginning of the unit, "How do plants help nature to keep her balance?" This group is a slow reading group and we read the selection orally for practice in pronunciation and because it was easier for the children to get the thought by hearing it. The reading for this group is often made real by using the collections of plant roots and leaves in the room. For example, we have in the room a specimen of rabbit bush, plant and root, which a group of boys dug up one weekend. After reading that plants in dry countries have long roots, which they develop in search of moisture, we stopped to discuss our twenty-foot root. At another place we read about the parts of trees. Librado was sent outside to bring in a section of a branch which had been pruned from a tree. By comparing it with the diagram in the book we located the heartwood, the sapwood, cambium layer, and bark. We noticed how cracked the bark was and found, by reading, that it was because the tree was growing. Toby suggested drawing a diagram of the parts of the tree so we could have it when we needed it.

During the time this group had been in the circle, I noticed several of the A group getting up to look for material. Antonio went to the encyclopedia. Ted had gotten several conservation bulletins and had leafed through them, probably reading very little. Juan, who likes to take short walks to the table and back to relieve nervous tension, was working hard and seemed to be doing some thinking. Angelita had finished her work and, going to the ant nest, wet the small cover cloth which provides moisture for the ants. Mary had gone over to Virginia to have her spelling dictated. These two girls have their own word lists, as they are very proficient spellers and do not work with any of the directed spelling groups.

Having concluded our discussion in the circle with the C group, I called the B group, giving them a few minutes to put their materials away while I went around checking and stimulating the group who were writing. I suggested that Ted take only one book at a time in searching for his information and showed him Reuben's paper which was partly finished and very good. Ted seemed to take this as a challenge. I made a mental note to make an appointment with him at noon so we could discuss better methods in getting his work done. Soilo was working spasmodically. Every once in a while he would rise and get a magazine, but he is overworked at home. He goes home from a hard day's work at school to do chores, spring plowing and planting and doesn't get enough rest and relaxation. He is a good thinker but he reflects his fatigue in school. Antonio was doing an excellent job of getting his material organized. He had used the encyclopedia and various bulletins, and such words from the word list as *infiltrate, runoff, terraces,* and *erosion.*

The B group in the circle had already begun to check their seatwork by reading sections from the book to prove their answers. When I went up Matilde was heatedly defending her answer. In discussion, we traced the routes of the Spanish and English pioneers. I asked, "Why didn't the Spanish explorers destroy as much of the natural resources as the English explorers?" Manuel said they had. This led us into a discussion which brought in factors of surface, climate, purposes of early colonists, use of land and its effect upon people today. As Angelita put it, "They weren't thinking of us." I asked, "Do you think people who settled in Nambé thought of future generations?" The children agreed that perhaps they hadn't and this brought us to the question, "What about us? Are we thinking about future generations?" Irene, who had been on a community land-use investigating committee last year, brought up the point of the amount of land and the increasing population and the practice of dividing land among heirs. Pita said, "If the land is poor, poor crops are raised and people don't have enough money to buy things they need." I prodded, "What are young people growing up now to do? Will they all live here in the valley?" As recess time was near I asked if they would like to keep on with the discussion. They were all interested in doing so and I asked if we could phrase a topic which we could keep in mind. We all agreed to think over and discuss for next time "Problems of Land Use in Nambé." We were to jot down all the ideas we could think of as well as ask our parents for the ones they thought important.

The prepared seatwork remained half-checked. I thought the interest and learnings brought out were more vital and necessary than finishing the assignment. We agreed to save it to be checked later.

After recess the children resumed their work. Tranquilino, from the sixth grade room, came for Sostenes. They are responsible for inspecting toilets and keeping them clean.

The B group was in the circle for directed reading. I passed some seatwork to the A group. The C group was getting busy on handwork, with the exception of Librado who was sitting with nothing to do but pull Mary's hair. I started him working on his multiplication combinations. Librado has very poor work habits and loses much of his time. He is poor academically and I give him as many opportunities to work in the shop as possible.

I passed out to the reading group four typed paragraphs with timed check-exercises. We have been doing this for some time to raise our reading speed. When these were finished I introduced a story, *Gray Goose*, about the exploits of a little girl during the Revolutionary War days. The children had some background for this, since during a previous unit on the present war we had discussed it. We tied it up by contrasting Spanish exploration, conquest, and independence with English. Also it was related to our social science discussion before recess. Before reading, several difficult words and phrases were introduced and explained. After a general comprehension check, we took up some questions which require specific reading and discussed vocabulary difficulties. I gave out seatwork, checking comprehension and vocabulary. The group was dismissed. It was twenty minutes of twelve, not enough time for another reading group. I suggested that since the two arithmetic groups had planned to take a short test we could spend our time doing so.

While the B reading group had been checking, Irene had gone to bring warm water for handwashing. The pupils at their seats had already washed their hands. At eleven-thirty, I excused two boys who went down to the primary school to help serve lunch to the lower grades. When the bell rang we had finished the test and those who hadn't washed their hands, now did so.

We went down to lunch. The children chatted naturally as they ate. Emily and Lola asked me for the key so they could sweep and tidy up our room before one o'clock. Joe Valdez went up to get the ball and bat; Abelino the basketball. The rest of the noon hour was spent in playing on the school grounds.

Our playground director asked if Soilo and Abelino could work planting iris on the terraces. I sent Abelino and Manuel. Soilo had been absent the day before and needed the work. I was particularly happy about Abelino's wanting to go because his previous attitude toward land use was one of ridicule. Now he wants to work on the grounds at every opportunity.

The A reading group was called to the circle. Those at their seats worked on wood carving, nursery school pictures, story reading, writing, arithmetic, reading, and social science seatwork. Emma, Lillie, and Basilia asked permission to go and meet with three others from the sixth grade and plan a picnic for the 4H Club. They had been delegated to do so during the last 4H Club meeting.

The same procedure was followed as before, tying up the selection with personal experiences and the community. There were a few difficult phrases which were introduced to this group before reading. A great deal of time was spent in reading and clearing up concepts. Seatwork was given out and the group dismissed.

Since everyone was working, I thought it best to go

around giving individual help. Antonio was checking some papers on computation fundamentals which had been handed in the day before. Adela was giving help to Dora and Odulia. After about half an hour of this individual checking, I called a low arithmetic group to the circle. This group had been working on fractions. Many of the pupils in this group, boys as well as girls, had experienced difficulty in measuring when they worked in the shop. This made the children realize their need for working with fractions. This group is working at a sixth grade level. Several of them are also working on multiplication as they are not up to standard.

We checked the day's assignment and gave a new assignment. The other group had been working on a problem scale test at their seats. We checked the test taken in the morning and worked on difficulties encountered. As this group finished checking, the recess bell rang.

After recess, each child worked individually. Joe painted on the mural; some took up their woodwork and carving; and Virginia was looking in science books for information about gophers. The day before a group had wished to know more about them and Virginia had volunteered to find the necessary information. Some worked on reading; some on arithmetic; some on words which had been misspelled in their writing. These were on the blackboard for one group. Another group (low) was to have directed work in the circle. Adela and Juanita worked by themselves using *Gates Common Spelling Errors,* a book listing common errors in children's spelling. Satisfying myself that

everyone was working, I called Antonio to check on his conservation story. His thoughts were very good, although his
spelling wasn't. We made a list of his misspelled words and
suggested a few revisions and additions. I commended him
highly. Next I checked Reuben's. He has the same difficulties as Antonio. His oral language is poor although he
doesn't hesitate in expressing himself. He experiences the
same difficulty in reading, being an excellent silent reader
and a poor oral one.

Reuben is in the remedial spelling group which emphasizes primarily the overcoming of language difficulties. He
expressed in his composition two exceptionally good
thoughts, "If we are to conserve our natural resources, people must be educated to it," and "Many people in Nambé
don't know enough about terracing and gully control but
the children are learning about conservation in school.
They go home and tell their parents and some of them practice these." I asked Reuben whether his father had changed
any of his farming practices because he (Reuben) had suggested it. He said he and his father had terraced the field
and had planted some cottonwoods near the river on their
land but these trees had been carried away by the flood.
Questioned further if he intended to plant any more, he
said he would like to put willows in and he'd like to plant
grass. But because people didn't care for their stock and let
them loose on the river bottom to graze on the scant vegetation, he didn't think it would be advisable unless people
got together and coöperated in controlling the stock.

I also got around to check Adela's paper. She was greatly

concerned with getting people to think of future generations. As she said, "We aren't the only ones who are to live on the land."

Juanita, a steadfast, consistent worker, was also doing a fine job with her paper. She, like Antonio, had gone to the encyclopedia and conservation bulletins and had gotten some highly technical information on soils. I suggested that she emphasize the side of land use that affects man rather than the technical side.

After all papers were checked, I called the remedial spelling group to the circle. Adela took care of dictating the spelling words to the other group. She collected the papers and checked them and put them upon my tray so I could look them over before handing them back. As she was doing this, we were having a lesson in phonics. We were using a reader designed especially for such remedial groups — *Improving Your Reading*. We had worked on beginning sounds, vowel sounds, and were taking up the pronunciation of longer words. We went around the circle giving each child a chance, and using sound clues to help with difficulties. One of the chief difficulties of this group is their inability to distinguish parts of words, especially the last part of words. They are still not proficient in solving word pronunciation and need much help.

As we finished, the bell rang and the group was dismissed. Everyone was putting his materials away. Several of the children were checking out magazines from Dora to take home. Laura and Toby were cleaning out their desks and when they finished setting things straight they got up and left. Sostenes wanted to stay and listen to the radio awhile. Toby came up to tell me he would not come to school tomorrow because he had to plant. I finally succeeded in getting him to come to school providing I would let him go early. A group of girls wanted to play a game of baseball. Lorenzo said he would umpire the game. Lillie checked out the Chinese checkers to take home.

With the help of the girls we got the room straightened out. I sat down to think over and plan tomorrow's work. Going over the day's work—

1. Lillie lost time today. I wonder why.
2. I must visit Librado's home, talk with his parents, and probably get a clue that will help me in reaching Librado.
3. Ted's problem.

I had a bulletin board to change. There were several pictures to change, words to be added to the word list. Go down to the office and talk with Mrs. Watson and see how the reading group is coming along. She will give me some suggestions for dealing with Librado. Ask her for any instructions. I collected my books to take home, to work on seatwork, charts, etc. I left at five-thirty.

Chapter 5

The Health Program in Nambé[11]

José Baca was dead. The church bell had been rung in the church on the hill. It had been rung slowly — a long peal every three minutes. Summoned by the wordless message of the bell the relatives and immediate friends of the family were gathered in the house where José had lived. They had come at the first sound of the bell for they had known José would die. He had been very sick for a week and when a man is sick enough to stay in bed a week it is inevitable that he die.

José lay in state in the living room in all the dignity and panoply that family, friends and church could give him.

José was dead — "Dios lo quiere" — God wills it.

José is but one of many in New Mexico.

New Mexico with a death rate of 13.8 has almost three more deaths per 1,000 of population than the nation at large. All of the ten counties, except one, having the highest death rates (from 14.7 to 22.1 per thousand) are counties where people of Spanish descent constitute more than half of the population.

---

11 This chapter was written from the reports and diaries of Mrs. Maria Casias Vergara, the Nambé nurse for two years, and from other staff diaries.

. . . Where the infant mortality rate for the nation is 51 for every 1,000 live births, the rate in New Mexico is 125.9. Thirteen of the counties have an infant mortality rate of less than 100, eighteen counties have rates ranging from 104.8 to 167! It is significant to note that the ten counties that have the highest infant mortality rates in the state are counties where more than half of the population is Spanish-speaking. . . . Health practices are often guided by medieval traditions and superstitions. These beliefs range from such matters as credence in the Evil Eye to faith in incompetent midwives and curanderos (herb doctors) — to say nothing of homely remedies, patent medicines, and general ignorance of modern health practices. Many of these people still live in the seventeenth century, insofar as matters of health are concerned. It is easy to understand why this is so. Modern health standards were developed in Western civilization after these people went into isolation. When the Spaniards came into New Mexico in the sixteenth and seventeenth centuries they came with the beliefs and standards of that time. Since then they have had no opportunity to learn of new developments in that field. They have, perforce, continued practicing the only standards they know. It is not at all remarkable that, being so far behind the times in health knowledge, these people should lag behind current trends in health status. Indeed, it would be remarkable if they did not. What is startling is that so little has been done to improve these conditions.[12]

THE HEALTH PATTERN OF THE VILLAGE

Very few exact records were available for Nambé proper. The following is a brief quotation from a report published in 1939:

---

[12] George I. Sanchez, *Forgotten People*, The University of New Mexico Press, Albuquerque, New Mexico, 1940, pp. 33-35.

The nearest hospital is in Santa Fe; the nearest doctor is in Espanola.

All but two families have a well. The depth to water in the wells varies from 20 feet when the irrigation reservoirs are full, to 60 feet when they are empty.

There have been several cases of malaria among the school children since 1934, and four cases of typhoid in the community.

The county nurse has recommended that cod-liver oil be given to 117 of the 153 children enrolled in the school, because they were definitely underweight. Altogether 3 dozen bottles were used during the spring of 1935.

Ninety per cent of the births are delivered by midwives, of which there are two in the community, neither being well trained.[13]

There was and is no trained physician in the community and little knowledge of or contact with clinics and hospitals in Santa Fe. A trip to Santa Fe is expensive and the cost of a visit from a physician is expensive. To use a local herb doctor is easier, cheaper, and customary.

The state health department physicians and nurses are few in number and have a tremendous territory to cover. Visits to any one community are few and far between. The public health nurse is the link between needy communities and medical service. But there are many needy communities in the Southwest and there are very few public health nurses. Sometimes she works in one or even two large counties.

The excellent work of the county nurses has been done

13 *Tewa Basin Study*, Volume II, Soil Conservation Service, Southwest Region, 1939, p. 7.

in spite of over-work and existing conditions. They can and do provide means of medical service and health education. They recognize the needs of the communities and they have worked and are working valiantly to meet them. But they cannot awaken the people to their own responsibilities and they cannot establish a complete program of health education because they *do not have the time.* The problems of these people cannot be solved by the limited services which the county nurses are able to provide. The little that they can do is often discounted a hundred times over by the things which they are expected to do and cannot.

Under such circumstances it is easier for the villagers to depend upon the local curanderos; the medico [14] who cures ailments by giving herbs or other self-prepared medicines, the salvador who specializes in massage of injuries, and — for deliveries — the midwife. The failure of these practitioners to restore health or relieve pain does not always destroy the people's faith in them. Usually the patients do not expect too much. But when they turn to the advice of trained doctors and nurses, when they subject themselves to clinics and hospitals, they expect immediate relief. When they do not always recover, or when a member of the family dies, in spite of all that trained medical aid could do, their faith is broken and the whole weary circle starts over again.

These people are sensitive and proud. They live in financial insecurity, which in turn makes for uneasiness. They

---

14 "Medico," as used in the manuscript, is a term used to designate the herb doctors and other non-medical healers of the community.

must be met with sympathy, understanding, and patience. One careless, harsh handling at a clinic will send them away forever. Like all of us, they must have trust and faith in a person before they will confide their troubles and place themselves in the hands of a stranger for treatment. Often a faith born of desperate hope is placed in the skill of a doctor or a nurse. If that faith is broken the old prejudices are built up again and the old bitterness returns.

Mothers of ten and twelve children, accepting the loss of two or three babies as the will of God, do not voluntarily turn for advice in saving their children, especially if the given advice is tempered with amusement at the number of children they have and disgust with the condition of the mothers themselves. Women of thirty, used to poverty and drudgery, have no idea that their lot could be made easier. It is the only life they know. Their one complaint is too many children — and in the isolated villages of the Southwest where the church binds family and community together, there is no tolerance of birth control. Nevertheless, these women are human. Their bodies are weaker than their minds and there are many criminal abortions which wreck the physical health and impair the mental health of the mothers.

Knowledge of modern nutrition, as of much modern science, was largely lacking. It is not improbable that in the early days before so much pressure was placed on the land the native diet was fairly adequate. But with the dwindling of resources, with the increase of population, with the loss of grazing land, with the disappearance of fish

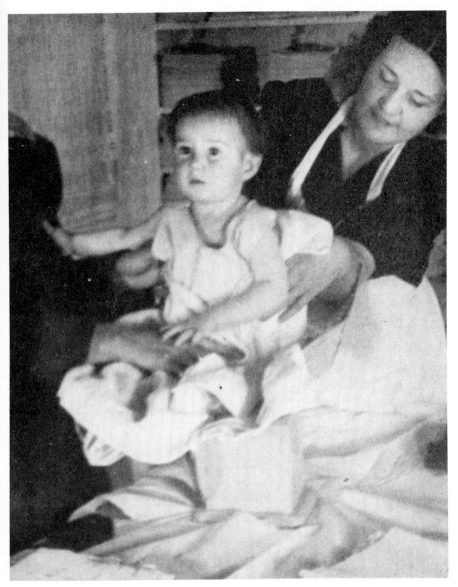

PLATE VII

A happy mother participates in the work of the clinic

PLATE VIII

The older brothers, who had left school, become interested in shop work. As a result they build an extra room

Photo Courtesy Soil Conservation Service

and game, and with the necessity for a certain amount of cash buying, diets became inadequate. The vitality of the population is low as evidenced by the vital statistics, by the large number of chronic colds, by fatigue and lack of endurance, by the incidence of communicable diseases.

Lunches which consisted of cold tortillas, sometimes spread with jelly, sometimes not — a cold potato, an occasional hard cooked egg, a slice of meat, a biscochita, or a store-bought cookie, are not adequate for a day of working and playing.

Starvation did not exist in Nambé, but poor nutrition did. The usual diet of beans, chili, tortilla, and coffee omits necessary milk and its products, fruits and vegetables, and whole grain products. On feast days and fiestas the diet may include soda pop and a cake with pink icing.

Through excellent work of the home demonstration agent canning was well established in the village. The women canned peas, corn, chili, squash, and fruits. There was a large supply of apples which lasted into the winter. Few of the mothers canned apples, however. They were dried in the sun and stored for winter. Potatoes, cabbage, and carrots were stored in underground pits for the winter months. Carrots from the gardens were eaten raw, they were seldom cooked. The more progressive mothers canned a variety of vegetables and varied the diet during the winter months with canned and dried fruits and canned meats. But these mothers numbered only a small per cent of all the women in the village.

The gardens were not large enough to meet the needs of

large families. The women used, to the best of their ability, the resources of the gardens in canning and the daily cooking of foods. But the vegetables were cooked until all the vitamin content was lost.

There were stores in the village where prices were high and credit was unlimited. But the majority of food purchases ran to baloney, white bread, cookies, and canned peaches.

THE PROBLEMS

Within a community of one hundred and ninety-four families were these problems, the origins lying in many cases deep in the customs, traditions, and superstitions of more than two hundred years. The problem of health and sanitation in the community could not be solved by a shelf of full medicine bottles or a drawer of waiting instruments and a doctor or a nurse on call. Nor could the work which we wanted to do — the education of the people to their own needs in health and sanitation — be done with only the weekly visits of an over-worked county nurse whose time was never long enough for the countless demands made upon it. The solution of our problem was not one of providing service alone. It was not one of monthly clinics. It was a problem of intensive health education.

It was a big job and we knew it. But we were willing to try. We set out to use the resources of the schoolrooms for the best means of health education that we could provide. We determined to work for the improvement of a program of health education which the county nurse, in spite of unbelievable odds, had initiated in the community. Accepting the aims of public health as the basic points of our program, we listed the immediate needs, as we saw them, in broad points:

1. Provision of better diets for the children by supplementing the school lunches, and by classes in cooking and nutrition.

2. Improvement of home living conditions through demonstration of sanitary wells and toilets, and instruction in the building of them.

3. Care of food and careful handling.

4. Development of good health and cleanliness habits; i.e., regular hours of sleep and rest, use of individual drinking cups, covering cough or sneeze with handkerchief, etc.; handwashing, bathing, teeth brushing, neatness in dress.

5. Prenatal care for expectant mothers, monthly examinations and provisions for the preparation of layettes; follow-up home calls by the nurse.

6. Infant Welfare clinics and follow-up calls by the nurse.

7. Education in proper care of babies after birth, feeding, cleanliness, proper rest (sleeping alone), etc.

8. Establishment of a clinic for testing of venereal diseases, and provision made for the attendance in the clinic at Santa Fe.

9. Treatment of eyes, teeth, and removal of tonsils of school children.

10. Prevention of some communicable diseases through immunization; quarantine of children with communicable diseases. Education of the people in isolation of communicable disease cases.

11. Control of the common fly, particularly as it affects babies and small children.

12. Personal hygiene emphasized by both teachers and nurses; home calls by teachers and nurse to aid in mental hygiene.

THE FIRST STEP

The first step was the initiation of a school lunch to supplement the diets of the children. The first attempt was a midmorning lunch served only to the children of the lower school. Milk was obtained from the WPA and supplemented with fresh fruit, crackers, or cereal. The lunch would have been impossible without the coöperation of the parents. They sent food donations (often bringing the food themselves) and gave a benefit dance to buy dishes for the school kitchen. The midmorning lunch was continued until the last two years of the project when the WPA established a lunch project in Nambé. During the last two years of the project a kitchen staff of five served a hot, well-balanced meal to the children of the upper and lower schools. But again, this program would have been nearly impossible without the coöperation of the parents. They sent cabbages, potatoes, and carrots from their winter stores. Mr. and Mrs. McCormick contributed vegetables, apples, and milk for the Nursery School. During the winter months it was not uncommon for a box of apples to be in every room. They were eaten during recess and after lunch (and behind geographies and story books).

The physical needs of the children were not the only concern of the staff. We did not intend to be satisfied with the provision of proper food and attention to physical defects. We knew that small bodies could not respond satisfactorily to care if small minds were tired and dulled by insufficient rest and poor home conditions. We realized that a health program conducted in the school alone would be superficial if home conditions were not considered. The health of our children was affected by outside circumstances such as heredity, home surroundings, and community environment. We knew that the answers to many problems of behavior and health were to be found, not only in physical examination of the children, but in the homes from which they came. In recognition of this fact, we accepted the responsibility of acquainting ourselves with every home in the community. We did not visit as home examiners, we visited as teachers, and through the years, as friends. Throughout the five years, one of the most valuable aspects of the program was the attention paid to the mental health of the children and adults. Home visits were not left to the nurse as her responsibility alone. They were considered a part of the teaching life of the staff.

During the first year of the project, the staff coöperated with the county nurse in the school program of public health. The children were examined and a thousand and one details were attended to every day. Impetigo was common during the first year. Through constant classroom teaching and through vigilance on the part of the teachers and the children (who were born detectives) sores were soon noticed, reported, and treated. Infected fingers were taken care of. The occasional dirty heads were washed until they were clean. The children became health conscious. Surrounded by examples of healthful living and preventative measures, they were quick to respond. The school rooms supported the health program by providing situations in which the children could learn and experience practices of good health. They were not reading about health practices from books, but were discovering in their every day living a better way of doing things. They washed their hands before lunch. They washed their hands when they returned from the toilet. They went to lunches of well-cooked food served on tables set with napkins and silverware and clean, individual dishes. They learned to eat foods they were not used to, first because these foods were good for them and later because they liked them. They learned to eat and demand fruit juices, vegetables, and green salads. They rested regularly, they drank quantities of milk, ate whole wheat bread — and they gained weight!

A healthy, clean, and happy atmosphere was provided for them and they responded beautifully. They worked in rooms with low furniture, ample shelf space and windows. They learned to sit where the light was best for protection of their eyes. The program was balanced between activities and written work. They knew they had the privilege of walking around to select books, of stretching, or of resting when they were tired. They listened to stories in the mornings and after lunch, and they learned to relax and rest during the story hour. They did not forget the habits they learned. They remembered health practices and put them to use. If they had sores on their hands they did not play with the clay. They drank from a sanitary drinking fountain and learned to safeguard and care for it. If their mouths were sore they asked for a drinking glass, spoon, and plate that would be kept entirely separate. They went to clinics confidently and they developed a desire for cleanliness.

The study of health was basic in the curriculum. Indeed, in a course of study based upon community needs and resources it was one of the most important phases, and from the first year the study of health developed into a consciousness of good health habits which was a part of everything the children did.

THE COMMUNITY NURSE

With provision for some of the immediate needs of the children, the staff turned to the immediate needs of the community. If we were to minister to the true needs of the community, if we were to effect the changes which were necessary, it would be necessary to employ a full-time nurse. We needed someone who could devote every day to the health needs of the people in our community. The program for which we were working was dependent upon constant effort and hard work. The education of the community was impossible through monthly meetings and monthly clinics — it was possible only through daily repetition and training.

In the fall of 1937, Mrs. Cyrus McCormick placed at our disposal a public health nurse whose duties would be confined to the village of Nambé. The nurse began her work in March of 1938. In the selection of a nurse for Nambé we wanted a person with sympathy, tolerance, and understanding. We needed someone who understood the people and their problems, who would work with them and for them — not at them.

Miss Maria Casias, the nurse chosen, was of Spanish extraction and spoke Spanish. She was a graduate not only of a nurse's training school, but had had public health training and excellent experience.

FACT FINDING

The first weeks of the nurse's work were spent in a community survey. She visited every house in the community. She used available records, but as these were incomplete she made a list of births and deaths, a record of home conditions and the needs of the families. The records which she made proved invaluable in the work which was done in the community and the school.

One end of a long, dark hallway was partitioned off and a window was knocked out of an adobe wall. The finished room was the clinic. Money for the clinic was provided by Mrs. McCormick, the health committee, and the U. S. Children's Bureau. But the significant fact of the Nambé health program was not that we had a clinic. It was that the nurse went from this clinic into every home in the community, and that the services which the clinic could provide were recognized and desired by the people of the community.

During the first year the kitchen, the office, the clinic, and the adjoining schoolroom were used for prenatal and infant welfare clinics. The Nambé public health nurse, working with the county nurse and the doctor, held monthly clinics. In addition to the clinics, the work of the nurse consisted of home visits, examination and care of the school children and constant checking of new babies, prenatal and post-partum cases; the teaching of classes in euthenics, first aid, cooking and nutrition, home and personal hygiene. An intensive and important part of her work, however, was the work she did with individuals. She was not concerned with the physical needs of the people alone, she was also concerned with their fears, their worries, their ambitions, and their happiness. There is a term for this. It is called mental health. We called it love for the children and interest in the people themselves.

Progress was not easy. Prejudice and ignorance were met with each step. There were a few irate fathers who followed the rules of naturopathics and whose opinion of the nurse and of medical doctors in general was entirely negative. And education of these individuals was imperative, as they were usually the ones who needed immediate medical aid for chronic diseases.

Often the nurse encountered direct opposition and discouragement. At times the medicos, or herb doctors, undid all that months of patient effort had accomplished. But it was not only the illiterate who shouted their antagonism in the face of the school and the nurse. Even the intelligent and progressive men were sometimes doubtful about methods or change. When the results were not quick enough or definite enough to satisfy them, they turned again to their local salvadores and so-called medicos.

At first the attendance at clinics was small. Mothers who had been accustomed to attendance and care only at the time of delivery of the baby, could not, at first, see the sense in attending a prenatal clinic every month. As far as they were concerned the attendance at one clinic should have been sufficient to assure a normal and safe delivery. Gradually, however, by word of mouth and with the constant aid of the nurse to mothers who were ill, whose new babies were losing weight because of improper diets, and the actual saving of babies whose lives were threatened, the mothers began to realize that here in the personage of a slender, dark-haired nurse was help to relieve their suffering and to improve the health of their children. As the months went by the nurse, with help and a sympathetic understanding of their problems, gained their confidence and their faith. They came to the clinics because they were confident that the nurse would be there to help them. Women who had ten children and saw no place of an eleventh on the income that was not sufficient for four persons, gained new courage in the simple fact that there was a way to have clothing ready for the new baby.

With the exception of a few scattered cases which show the deepness and the strength of the superstitions and prejudices with which we had to deal, there was no direct opposition to the program. The people had been so long without sufficient aid, they had so many children and so little money, and they needed so many things that the first thing they wanted was material aid. Their main desire was immediate and bountiful help.

To quote from the nurse's diary:

During the first year of the health program in Nambé, it was extremely hard to initiate a program of education because the people wanted material help and not educational advancement.

It became increasingly evident that the time had come for more community participation.

THE HEALTH COMMITTEE

To reach the people of the community and make them aware of the problems as their own, to gain their coöperation and aid, a health council of ten laymen, the nurse, and the principal was formed. The health committee held its first meeting on February 1, 1939. At the first meeting it was decided to meet monthly.

The following program was sponsored by the community:

1. Coöperation with the nurse and the school in health education in the community.
2. Raising of funds for the correction of children's health defects (eyes, tonsils, and teeth).
3. Discussion of community problems with the nurse and the school.
4. Coöperation with state and county agencies.

The actual working of the committee is shown in the following two excerpts from the nurse's diary:

The necessity of people furnishing their own transportation to doctors was discussed at the committee meeting. Much of the nurse's time is wasted furnishing unnecessary transportation when she could be serving the community in more valuable ways. One member of the committee had been quite provoked with the nurse because she refused to furnish him transportation. The other committee members argued with him in favor of the nurse.

The condition of the toilets in the community was discussed. Mr. McCormick suggested that the people start working on the improvement of toilets. The committee decided to start with the church toilet as soon as Father Salvadore returned from Rome.

Other problems discussed and explained in the meeting this month were:

1. Duties of the physician and the nurse.
2. Causes of diarrhea — open toilets and flies.
3. Urgency of having materials in hand for layettes for mothers who do not have money to buy them. (Committee gave money for this purpose.)
4. Explanation of the complications of defective tonsils, teeth, and eyes.
5. Discussion of medical doctors, chiropractors, osteopathic doctors, and naturopathics. An important point was brought out — "It is unethical for a doctor in good standing to advertise himself."

During the first year of the committee's organization over one hundred and forty dollars was raised through movies, benefit dances, plays, and contributions. The money was used for tonsillectomies, refractions and glasses, dental extractions, flannel for layettes, and the construction of a sanitary privy for the church. The construction of the privy, after months of effort on the part of the nurse and her health committee, was a crowning achievement, for there is a definite connection between insanitary privies and flies, diarrhea, and infant deaths.

The education of the community was not entirely the sole responsibility of the nurse and the teachers. The children carried new learnings into the homes, and often their words were followed and their rebukes were listened to when the words of others fell on deaf ears. From the diary comes the story of a firm six-year old:

Maybe the older people don't believe in germs, but our six-year olds know differently. Juan B. Rivera was telling me about six-year old Gloria who refused to drink water from her sister's drinking glass. Her sister has been sick in bed with the flu. She told her parents she would catch what Frances had if she used her dishes.

During the toothbrush campaign, held soon after the arrival of the nurse in the community, it was the children who initiated the use of toothbrushes in the homes; and the nurse and the children unwittingly educated the village storekeepers too. There was a demand for toothbrushes and the storekeepers had to purchase them to keep up with competitors. Again, when the nurse told the mothers to wash their baby's clothes in a certain kind of soap flakes, the storekeepers were asked to obtain the soap flakes for the customers.

The matter of health education in the classrooms was not only a matter of toothbrushes and learning about germs, however. The classrooms supported the health program of the nurse by providing situations in which the children could learn and experience practices of good health. In the lower grades, experience charts provided reading material of the children's compositions about the fly, proper food, safety, cleanliness, good manners, and personal hygiene. In the upper grades, microscopes tested well water and river water. The children studied sanitation and wells, the causes of disease, proper foods, and means of preventing illness and providing good health.

They applied the things they learned to practical use — the health of their classmates and the sanitation practices of the school were accepted as their responsibility. During a study of water, the fourth and fifth grades observed the new well was being dug below the toilets. They were concerned until they were informed the toilets would be moved.

A record was kept on every child in school, and the teachers used these individual records constantly in working with the children. Height and weight charts were kept in every room, and the loss or gain of each child was noted and investigated. The teaching practices and the classroom supported the health program.

Success With the Children

The most satisfactory results of the whole program were in the children. We watched their growth, we checked the difference in attitude and behavior after bothersome tonsils and teeth had been removed. We ministered to their everyday needs — the bloody noses (Nambé boasted hardy pugilists), the skinned knees, the headaches, and the stomach aches. We had, in return, their confidence and trust. There were so many little things they did and said that all added up to a successful health program. There was the time a six-year old boy sat in one corner of his family's three roomed house and demanded the nurse. He glared until his family sent for her. There were the countless times grimy little boys with dirty ears and three-cornered grins brought a bar of soap for the handwashing and proffered it saying, "It smells nice." The teachers were their friends and the security of their school world, but the nurse was a creature set apart. She was pretty. She helped them when they needed her, and they never forgot her. But the value of an integrated classroom and school health program was shown when they turned, after she left, to other nurses with confidence and to the classroom study of health with interest. They had seen health measures in practice, in the classrooms they had learned the need for health of every person and they had worked and played with recognition of health habits. The teachers and the nurse and children, working together, had gained a basic foundation in healthful living.

Special Classes

Every week the nurse met with classes in first aid, eugenics, cooking and nutrition, and personal hygiene. These classes were continued through the summer months, as were the clinics and the daily work of the nurse. For the first time the younger married mothers and the girls of high school age were given opportunity to learn that the old superstitions and prejudices which they, children of a new generation, were doubting were without basis or truth. In their place they were given facts, knowledge, and the opportunity of learning to put the new health practices into actual work. These were not theoretical dissertations on health but practical demonstration and the working out of individual health problems. The summer work proved one of the most valuable parts of the program. The greatest part of the work done was accomplished through the coöperation of the younger mothers and the high school girls. They were interested and hungry for knowledge which they could use in their own homes and in the homes of their parents. They asked that the classes be continued and they brought their questions and their problems to be discussed with the nurse.

There is not space to include the full reports for the years of 1938-1940 which show in figures the tremendous amount of work that was accomplished by the Nambé nurse, the county nurse, the doctors who assisted at the clinics, and the coöperating agencies. But even these reports do not include the endless transporting of patients to clinics, the countless visits made in rain and snow across the river and up the arroyos. There is no mention of the toothbrush campaign, the endless battle against skin diseases, and countless other improvements. They do not record the weekly run of the station wagon to the venereal clinic in Santa Fe, they make no mention of the velorios the nurse attended, the many community functions and problems which the staff and nurse participated in — and which were regarded, not as a part of their work, but as a part of living in the community.

More than figures, the reports from the nurse's diary recording the second year show the progress which was being made in the community:

In my home visits lately, I have noticed a great change in attitudes. People are so very friendly. It is really genuine. At first they were courteous, convinced in very few ideas. Now they are ready to believe most advice given. Yesterday while giving advice of diet to a postnatal she explained that she had never eaten fruit after delivery, but if I advised it she would eat it.

Mothers seem to have become more interested in the proper diets for their children. They have much faith in Dr. Lathrop and his teachings. When the nurse goes to see them they don't ask about laxatives so much, they are beginning to learn the value of fruit juices.

And from the diary, comes the story of the old methods and superstitions in opposition with the new:

I went in to see —— ——- today. He has been very sick and is still having much abdominal distress. While I was there they arrived with mercury. They told me that mercury was good for constipation. The grandmother told me that they were doing the things I wanted them to do — following the doctor's directions, and also doing some of the treatments that they believe in doing. The following are the words the grandmother used:

"We give the patient up to God, then we try our medicines and treatment, which probably are not very good because we know nothing about science. If it is the Lord's will our patient gets well."

The baby's mother, however, was relying more upon the instructions left by the doctor than upon the advice and beliefs of her mother.

Once more from the diary is the following list of achievements not to be found in any statistical report:

We have convinced the mothers of the importance of the following information and use of it:

1. Cleanliness
2. Regularity — feeding and sleeping
3. Flies cause diarrhea — the Evil Eye does not
4. The importance of tomato juice and orange juice
5. Immunizations
6. Boiled water for babies
7. The importance of the baby sleeping alone in a separate crib protected from flies with a netting

The following are teachings accepted by many of the villagers:

1. Fluids for fever
2. Alcohol rubs to reduce fever
3. Enemas to reduce fever and distention
4. Rest in bed
5. Aspirin will dull pain, but will not cure the disease.
6. Last year at this time many people from Nambé were going to a naturopathic doctor. At present I know of no one going.
7. In many classes children have been taught personal hygiene.
8. They learned that good doctors do not advertise.
9. The mothers believe in binding their legs for varicose veins and in elevation several times daily for better circulation.

A most valuable work accomplished by the nurse was the education of the mothers in better baby and child care. Cribs were built in the shop, made to specifications that insured ample room for the baby and not enough room for another child to sleep with the baby. The mothers accepted teachings in proper diets and sanitation. They made layettes and equipped baby trays — but most important of all, the mental health of the mothers was much better during pregnancy and after the arrival of the baby than it had ever been before.

THE CARRY-OVER

Although the full-time services of the nurse were terminated in September, 1941, through lack of funds, and the community had only nursing service available to other communities, the effect and carry-over were definite.

The younger married mothers regularly attended the clinics conducted by the county nurse. They came for advice and for aid in caring for their children. The people came to the school to use the phone to call a doctor, they asked for grapefruit and fruit juices when their children were ill. Every Wednesday the clinic station wagon carried patients to the venereal clinic in Santa Fe. Children were sent to school early in the morning to be transported to dental and eye clinics. The parents, with the aid of the county public health nurse and the school, were beginning to accept the responsibility of their children's health. Instead of accepting illness as caused by the "Evil Eye or the will of God" they asked for aid in caring for their children, and instances such as the one reported from a teacher's diary were numerous:

Mrs. Romero sent a note today, saying that she thought Carrie needed glasses as she was having "pains in the head" and her eyes hurt. She asked when Carrie could be examined and how much the glasses were.

Due to excellent work by the county public health unit and the extensive social work of principal and teachers and the classroom education, the health program in Nambé continued to function and to prove of value. The end of the five years found a basic study of health in every classroom in the school. At the end of five short years the community was aware of its own problems and of the fact that health conditions could be remedied through its own efforts. The two and one-half years of intensive public health work in one community did not benefit that community alone. Through the great effort and interest of Mrs. Cyrus McCormick a second public health nurse was secured for the county of Santa Fe, and the Santa Fe County Health Committee was organized. What had seemed impossible became a reality. The special piece of work at Nambé had resulted in permanent benefit to the entire county. And we, of Nambé, sincerely believe that the program, brief as it was, was to prove of lasting value. We are able to list achievements that had been beyond our greatest hopes: an improvement in community health conditions — and the first step toward a county health program of larger scope and opportunity.

Chapter 6

Co-operation and Participation

A community school program does not spring full grown from dreams but evolves from years of patient and persistent toil. Five years or ten years are not long enough to develop the program of the ideal community school. But in five years there is time to develop the friendliness and neighborliness with the community which any school should have.

A new school building can be constructed from the blueprints of an architect. The program that is proposed for the school can be planned by a curriculum specialist. But no one can construct the wholesome and successful working together of the teaching staff, the children, and the people. The human qualities of kindliness and sympathy, of helpfulness and understanding, can not be drafted into the school building. These things have to grow from within a community. They can be identified by many terms — they can be called community coöperation and participation. But it is very difficult to describe the spiritual qualities which helped to build a school program in words from a dictionary. The intangible things which made the Nambé school part of good living and which provided inspiration for each day's work cannot be justified by cold terms. There is no one expression which will do justice for the time Henry Ortiz wired the carpenter shop for us; the time Abel Ortiz deeded the school a piece of property for a school well; the time Celestino Ortiz donated land for a school garden; or the time Seferino Lujan said, "I won't be able to come to the meeting — but you can count on me for any help you need." The term "participation" cannot record, in itself, the countless times the fathers stopped to chat in passing by the school, or all the times we walked down the road in the evening, exchanging a weary greeting with the people as we passed — laughing with them as they said, "Mucho trabajo — no dinero."

Yet these are the things — call them facts or records — which make this chapter, for they were as much the work of the staff and the people as the planning of the classroom routine or all the community meetings. The most important phase of the work in Nambé was not only in planning a curriculum and carrying it out; it lay in meeting the community and becoming acquainted with the people, in discovering their needs, and in redirecting the school program to help them to meet their needs.

It was this part of the work which required time — not the time of a working day, but time reckoned in months and years; for it is not possible to go into a community that has known the same blood and the same family names for generations and say, "Now we are going to have a community school." The act of smiling cheerfully and remarking that "we will all coöperate" will not build a school which is an integral part of the community. You do not use the term "we" until you are a part of that community, and you cannot become a part of that community until you have fought the people's battles with them, worried with them, argued with them, worked with them, danced at their fiestas and celebrated at their weddings and attended their funerals as a friend — genuinely sincere. Until you are considered a member of that community there will be no coöperation with you. It makes little difference whom you may represent or what work you may do, there can be no coöperation with your aims and the aims of the people until the people are sure for what you, as a person, are working. And no work can be accomplished until each of you understands and accepts your responsibility in working with each other. Then the coöperation, if it is sincere, will not be thought of in terms of "coöperation." It will be a deep, strong neighborliness — and it will not begin and end with each new idea; it will go on through every day of the year.

The work of the Nambé staff during the first year of the project consisted in becoming acquainted with the people and conditions in the community. During all the five years the staff tried to make a place for the school where it could serve the best advantages of the people and become an integral part of community coöperation.

There had been coöperation in the village long before the idea of the community school was conceived. The people had lived by coöperation — it was the backbone of their existence. They had not realized that this coöperation, strengthened by some material aid and applied in the right places, could achieve other than immediate community needs.

The united effort of the villagers could not bring them the security or the independence they once knew. Some of these problems are too big for any small group: unemployment, loss of resources, sickness, poverty, and isolation. The villagers have always considered as their responsibility the welfare of neighbors, the upkeep of the church, the irrigation ditches, all of the community institutions. But because the school was established and kept up by the county they had never considered it an integral part of community responsibility.

Organized community coöperation in regard to the school began to assume larger proportions when Mr. and Mrs. McCormick bought the site of the old school building as part of their property and, in payment, contributed to a new school building higher on the hill, across the road from the community church. When the two Nambé school buildings were consolidated and another was built through community effort, aided by material help from the McCormicks and the WPA, the first step was taken toward the realization that the old conditions could be changed for the better. But there was still much to be done. The people knew little of the opportunities offered by federal and state agencies. They needed aid to save their land from wasting away; they needed opportunities for grazing lands now shut off; they needed a better understanding of the services offered by the Public Health Department; many of them needed employment and the chance to better their living conditions. Organized community coöperation had built a school building and voted for a more extensive program of education. The program which had been planned for the new community school would have to strengthen that community coöperation and serve as a connecting link between the people and the numerous agencies which could assist them.

THE PEOPLE AND THE SCHOOL

In the fall of 1935, two years prior to the opening of the Nambé Community School, an organization, comprised of parents and teachers, was started in the community. The organization was not affiliated with the national Parent Teachers Association, but it had been organized for the purpose of bringing the parents and teachers together. It was through this organization that much of the work in Nambé was accomplished during the five years of the project.

In order to reach all the people of the community, or their representatives, monthly meetings of the so-called PTA were held. Some of the meetings were for the purpose of business only, while others were for entertainment and business. The immediate aim of the staff was to interest and help the parents to recognize and assume the responsibility for their part in the school program. Plans were made in the meetings and new proposals explained; desires were expressed and discussed, and troubles or grievances were aired. In every case the friendly spirit of the staff and of the people was evident. The two languages of Spanish and English, interpreted when necessary, the appointment of committees, the group singing, and the feeling of people quietly accepting responsibilities and working out problems and plans together, served to weave into more of a whole the school staff and the people of the community.

Coöperation in a community is dependent upon the commonness or unity of purpose among citizens. If the river overflows its banks, everybody turns out and works prodigiously; if the irrigation ditches need cleaning and repairing, all the interested men contribute their services. It does not follow, and indeed is not true, that everybody will be interested in every aspect of community life. But if the citizens in a community have the same hopes and ambitions, a unity of purpose exists and the development of coöperation is possible.

In villages such as Nambé, which have been continuously occupied for centuries, there exist many cliques which hold differences of opinion with tenacity and, sometimes, ferocity. The division of water, political affiliation, property rights, and grazing rights are illustrations of the causes which may make dissension. And while these differences of opinion do not directly affect the school, the small feuds which they engender have a demoralizing effect upon the coöperation of the community as a whole.

If there is to be no regimentation in a democracy, there must be differences of opinion. Always there is a minority which does not agree with the decisions of the majority, and even in a community of six hundred people there will not

always be unanimous coöperation. This fact does not necessarily destroy a program of community planning, for if
there is a common meeting ground, the people will meet,
and through meetings and open discussion differences
which arise will be smoothed out. This is the American
way of life. It was true of Nambé. The staff did not hope
for the coöperation of each and every individual in the
community; they only expected to receive the coöperation
of the majority. They felt that the existence of both a majority and a minority group held more promise for the
growth of the school as a community responsibility than an
apathetic acceptance by all members. If people were interested enough to argue in the meetings they were interested
in the future of the school.

THE DEVELOPMENT OF THE COMMUNITY PROGRAM

As we gathered in more and more of the older boys who
were over-age we found an acute need for a wood-working
shop. The NYA offered to provide a teacher if we could
provide the building. We presented the matter to the parents. Men volunteered to help make adobes, or to lay them,
and the women volunteered to plaster the walls. The Forest
Service gave the "vigas" and the school paid for the windows and the hardware. The report of the actual construction of the shop is found in the principal's diary:

The carpenter shop is actually on the way as the men are
busily engaged in making the adobes for the walls of the building. The adobes are being made at Mr. Henry Ortiz's, just
across from the school. When the making of the adobes was

discussed, Mr. Ortiz said, "I think we should not make the adobes on the school ground as we would have to use Mr. Mc-Cormick's water. We can make them at my place and haul the water from the ditch. It is not fair to abuse the friendship of Mr. McCormick by using his water when we can get it from the ditch just as easily. We do not want to take advantage of kindness."

Mr. Abel Ortiz took his team and plowed the land yesterday. Lorenzo Rivera helped him break up the earth for the adobes. This morning Henry Ortiz hauled the straw and water before he drove his bus route. Six men are engaged in the actual work of making the bricks. If all goes well they should be made today.

. . . Yesterday's accomplishments were excellent. Seven hundred and fifty adobes instead of the estimated 600. Six men worked until noon today and completed 1,076 bricks. This number will be sufficient to build the walls and probably complete the walls around the privies.

Several men promised to help in whatever way they could; some offered to haul rock, some wanted to help lay the walls. . .

. . . The wind blew terribly today, yet in spite of all the bad weather Mr. Fred Salazar hauled six loads of rock and sand for the carpenter shop. He was so glad to do his share. He said that when we were ready for the roof he would be very glad to come and help.

Eventually this shop was too small. The government offered to provide a training course for fifteen men and girls in woodworking if quarters were available. Again the parents were consulted. They offered their assistance, but this time most of the work on the additional room was done by the boys who had joined the classes. The shop not only provided employment for out-of-school youths, it also served as an opportunity for fathers who wished to work in the evenings. In the shop many screen doors, cribs, and articles of furniture for the homes were made, as well as needed school equipment. Most important of all, there was the beginning of a pattern here — the need of the people for the shop, the school's recognition of the need, the contacting of government agencies, and the coöperation of the agency, the people, and the school to construct the shop.

During the second year of the project the pattern deepened. The people were beginning to realize the importance they held as a working influence in the life of the school:

The Nambé school has electric lights in the lower building! This makes a long-time dream a reality. Perhaps by and by they will be installed in the upper building.

The entire cost of the lights was around $25. This amount was paid by the PTA. The people are so pleased to know that the fund is being used to promote permanent improvements in and around the school.

And the people began to take much more of a part in the meetings. Instead of only one or two spokesmen for a meeting, several parents would voice their opinions:

. . . The matter of the dance dispensed with, two of the men sang a lengthy song, then the people called upon Mr. Lujan to make a speech. He made one of the best impromptu talks I have heard for some time. He urged parents to send children to school every day so that the boys and girls might have the opportunities that were being offered to them. He also stated clearly the purpose of the PTA, namely, to unite parents and teachers in their efforts to work together for the best interests of the boys and girls of the community.

The pride in their school was not expressed by flattery or praise. It was, instead, evident in friendly acts such as the times Mrs. Sofia Romero lent us her team and wagon, or the time Ramon Montoya offered to help Lorenzo, the recreational director, start the work on the terraces. And there was a gracious gesture of pride and neighborliness in the way mothers sent slips and seeds for the school flower beds.

The activities of the people, working as the PTA, were numerous. When dishes were needed for the school lunch the parents gave a dance, sold cakes and cookies, and bought the equipment for the kitchen. A library committee was responsible for the distribution of books and magazines. During one summer a playground committee took charge of the grounds on Sundays, tools were purchased for the carpenter shop, and the equipment for eight swings was provided. The balanced lunches which were served, with the coöperation of the WPA, would have been impossible without the food donations of the parents. During one month, the parents donated (and the children consumed) 65 quarts of milk, 138 pounds of cabbage, 240 pounds of carrots, 40 pounds of beans, 105 pounds of onions, 20 pounds of pears, 162 pounds of potatoes, 10 pounds of rice, 12 pounds of squash, 33 pounds of sugar, and 9 pounds of tomatoes. During the last year of the project the people raised $142 through donations and benefits for the construction of a school well. The well was drilled and installed by WPA labor. The electric pump was donated by Mr. and Mrs.

McCormick. Here again was the pattern of the people, the school, and the agency working together.

The value of the PTA was strengthened by the friendliness and the neighborliness which was developed through the daily contacts of teachers and parents. A friendly talk over a fence, or a cup of coffee after school with a mother or a father will mean more than any two-hour meeting ever could. There is not space to include a narrative report of all the human relationships which built the school program and kept it going. It is possible to list only a few of the instances and hope that the reader, by multiplying these many times, will be able to visualize the working together of the teachers and the people — and feel some part of the quality of friendliness and neighborliness.

During vacation the teacher, who assumed responsibility for the cooking program, spent considerable time writing out recipes for her landlady. Prior to and during the vacation, the teacher sent her different foods which she had prepared. The entire family enjoyed the food to such an extent that her landlord demanded that his wife learn how to cook similar foods. He and the children were tired of tortillas and chili and beans. He even asked his wife to cook a turkey with dressing. She had never cooked a fowl in the oven, having always fried all her meat. The teacher taught her how to dress, stuff, and bake the turkey. She also taught her how to prepare cranberries, a dish called for by the five-year-old daughter who had eaten them for the first time in nursery school.

This morning I visited our gully — the stretch of deeply eroded land on Mr. Salazar's land which the eighth grade boys have adopted as their project. They have been placing branches from the school trees in the gully after each pruning to see if the branches will hold the soil which is washed down with each rain. I noticed that the branches had held six inches of soil, keeping it from being washed on down the field. Mr. Salazar was so pleased with our efforts that he has promised to fence the plot. This will keep the cattle from eating the vegetation we have planted to prevent the soil being washed or blown away.

Tonight Mr. Montoya borrowed the pressure cooker. He and his wife are packing meat. He offered to pay rent, but he was told there was no charge. He remarked, "I do appreciate this offer, and perhaps we can help you in some way."

In Nambé, as in every community, there were community and church organizations which constituted an important part of community life. The people were gracious in extending their help to meet the needs of the teachers and the school. In turn, the teachers became more a part of the village life by recognizing their responsibility to community organizations and by participating in the plain fun of community functions. They went to fiestas and weddings, they assisted in planning programs and celebrations. The annual community Christmas Pageant became the responsibility of the staff and the Community Pageant Committee.

The annual S.P.M.T.D.U. (fraternal organization) program was held last Saturday. The weather was perfect and the parade was better than last year in that there were many more horses and riders and fewer cars. The children rode in three large trucks and each truck was driven by a member of the organization. The whole program was interesting and the dance was a big success.

. . . At nine this morning there was an annual mass for two

women. The women were closely related to several of the children. . . . Both the priest and the parents were happy to see the children ushered into the pews by their teachers. One father said to me — "I am happy you take the children to church. Don't excuse them to go by themselves as they just play. Unless you take the children we would rather they would be in school with you."

Mr. Seferino Lujan came late last night and asked for a room in which to hold a political meeting. He was given the lamps and the keys to the school building.

. . . This morning Abel Ortiz asked for a room to hold an election to vote bonds for the new county courthouse. Part of the auditorium was arranged for him and the election was carried on without any confusion to the school.

The school buildings became the center for community functions, but they came to mean more than mere community meeting places. As the years passed and the pattern of coöperation continued to deepen, the school was recognized as the place where assistance and help were available. The men came to the school for help in writing letters of application, the women came to the school to sew, to bring their babies to the clinic, to ask for recipes and slips from the school plants. As the people realized that the school could and would help them secure the aid they often needed from the clinics and the welfare departments, they came to ask advice about the agencies, to secure information in regard to NYA and WPA employment. Through the school's use of agencies, the people became aware of them, and the constant effort of the staff to contact agencies and bring them into the school program was strengthened as the years went by. The school became the link between the people and the channels of living from which they had been isolated for so long, and the people began to make use of the existing opportunities.

Henry Ortiz stopped by the school this morning and said he was taking the funds raised by the health committee to Santa Fe to be matched by the Children's Bureau. He wanted to know exactly where to go and how much explaining he would have to do. Henry is a leader in the community and is very respected by all the men.

THE CO-OPERATING AGENCIES

The functional program of the community school was dependent upon assistance of the numerous agencies and organizations. Without the interest and understanding of the individuals who represented the various agencies, many phases and achievements of the program would have been impossible. The greatest value of the program of the coöperating agencies is that the use of their services was not unique to Nambé. It was the utilization of the resources which are available to *every* public school in the country, if the staff is willing to contact these agencies and use the assistance they are able to give. Yet such a service program cannot succeed unless the people have been awakened to the need of such help.

Wise use of the land was constantly emphasized in the classrooms and in community contacts. It was only natural that the land program should be carried out with advice and assistance of the representatives of the Soil Conservation Service. Grass seed, seedlings, drought-resisting plants for the school grounds and school projects, directions in practices of soil conservation, printed and visual material for classroom and community use were all made available to us. It was through the constant guidance and support of the agents of this service that the school was able to bring the needs of proper land usage to the attention of the community and to teach several of the farmers simple land practices. In the spring of 1942, Nambé became a part of a Soil Conservation District. Inclusion in the district was due to the efforts of several local men who worked constantly for it. But the coöperation which made the establishment of the district possible rests upon the general recognition by the community of the fact that the land needed attention and assistance was available.

Again, through the Extension Service of the State Agricultural College, the school received assistance from the county agricultural agent and the home demonstration agent. A 4H Club was organized; demonstrations in the care of foods and gardens were given. Through the efforts of the home demonstration agent a Nature Study Club was organized and an interest was stimulated in block printing and leather work. One of the most valuable phases of the work of the home demonstration agent was the establishment of canning in the community prior to the opening of the community school. During one year an abandoned home was turned into a mattress factory where much needed mattresses were made by the mothers of the community.

The county agricultural agent helped with pruning of the trees. He went to the mountains with the older boys for evergreen trees and assisted in their planting and care. Every spring he gave the boys and girls who had gardens, onion plants and garden seeds and coöperated with the school program of utilizing land resources.

Through the services of the Forest Service we were able to secure evergreen trees to plant on the school grounds and to make use of many excellent educational opportunities, such as movies, lectures, lantern slides, and literature.

The WPA and NYA have been constantly referred to in this chapter. The WPA was responsible for many of the additions to one building. Our recreational leader was provided by it, as was the hot lunch. In September of 1938 the WPA Nambé Nursery School was established. During the five years of the program the NYA woodwork project provided work for the out-of-school youths and, whenever possible, secretarial help for the staff.

The health program in Nambé, described in detail in Chapter V, depended upon the aid of the Santa Fe County Health Department, the State Welfare Department, the Maternal Clinic, the Catholic Clinic, and the Dental Clinic in Santa Fe, and the resources offered by the Carrie Tingley Hospital.

In addition to these, the staff made constant use of the public library in Santa Fe and the 4H Club and Extension Service of the New Mexico State Agricultural College for literature which was used by both the children and the adults of the community.

Five years were not enough to see the full development of the program of the community school and the coöperating agencies, but the foundation was laid. The children realized the importance of the agencies and were fully aware of their existence. The people realized that the agencies existed for their use. By constant effort on the part of the teaching staff and by the individuals who represented the agencies, a groundwork was established that we hoped would not be destroyed when the project was ended. A way was opened for the people to make the best use of community and state resources. Progress is always slow, and the continued use of the agencies will depend upon the vigilance of the community leaders and the strength and direction of community coöperation.

Chapter 7

Evaluation

INTRODUCTION

Evaluation is an integral part of any program. This duty has been recognized by the staff from the very first day. Units of work have been scrutinized with care and modified in many respects. Diaries have been kept by every teacher. Detailed outlines of work were made.

For an even more detailed study it was decided to give especial attention to the whole program of evaluation during the fourth year. By this time our children had been with us long enough to show some effect from our program, and one year remained of the five years in which to make such corrections as seemed necessary.

Should we test basic skills? Yes, for although we did not give them primary emphasis we still expected the children to acquire reasonable proficiency in their use. Should we test knowledge of land management and practices? What about health? We had endeavored to develop individual responsibility. Had we been successful? Had we helped in the matter of coöperation? Is there actual evidence in the classrooms of children's interest in conservation or that we are using community resources? Would a visitor detect any different attitude in our children than in any other school? Are the individual interests of the children receiving attention?

COMMITTEE EVALUATION

We finally decided to make up an evaluation booklet patterned after the Evaluation Charts used by the North Central Association to study secondary schools; then we would invite a competent committee to spend a day with us and decide how well we were doing what we claimed we were doing.

Evaluation Committee

Mrs. Eunice Adams, Elementary School Supervisor, Bernalillo County.

Mr. Ed Bahr, Curriculum Department, New Mexico State Department of Education.

Miss Frances Carey, Principal, Elementary School, Santa Fe.

Mr. Joe Granito, Superintendent of Santa Fe County Schools.

Mr. B. Linthicum, Principal, Elementary School, Albuquerque.

Mrs. Ruth Logan, Elementary School Supervisor, Sandoval County.

Professor H. W. Sininger, Professor of Education and Director of Teacher Training, Highland University.

Miss Marjorie Large, Instructor in Education, Highland University.

Schedule, March 6, 1941

8:45   Preliminary meeting.
9:15-3:00   Visitation in classrooms to study the work.

3:00-5:00   Meeting of evaluation committee to prepare re-
            port.
5:00-6:30   Dinner at the school.
6:30-8:00   Meeting of evaluation committee with Nambé
            staff for presentation and discussion of report.

Instructions to the Committee

This evaluation represents no attempt to secure blanket
approval of everything we are doing. You are asked to
report evidence that may exist, or point out deficiencies in
respect to certain phases of our program. We are not asking
for full appraisal of our success in teaching the three R's,
for that will be done by a standardized testing program.
However, the point is included so you may express your
general opinion of the situation in this respect.

1. Each teacher has prepared a brief description of the pupils
    in his room, background of present work and his aims.
    This will be on the teacher's desk.
2. Consider the community, grounds, the equipment, the
    pupils, the curriculum, the teachers, in making comments.
3. The information necessary to judge certain items has been
    gathered in Mrs. Watson's office.
4. Remain in your assigned room until you have gathered
    evidence. Be definite and concrete as to good and bad
    points with sufficient detail to support your notation.
5. Rate each item 1-5. Consider 5 best. Add to the list as
    necessary. Write the teacher's name at the top.
6. Every piece of children's or teacher's work in the rooms
    is since February 1 or later. (Some within two weeks).
7. Your booklet will be turned over to Mr. Tireman at the
    close of the day.

8. Tenure. Mrs. Watson, Mr. Angel, Miss Ortiz, four years. Mrs. Ford, Mrs. Sanchez, two years. Miss Pfeister, Miss Wyss, Miss Armijo are here their first year.

On file in the principal's office will be detailed information in regard to the following:

1. The A.D.A. for each four years.
2. Total amount of community contributions — food.
3. County, state, federal agencies contributing.
4. Minutes of Council meeting.
5. Minutes of PTA meetings.
6. Report on nurse's activities.
7. Copy of programs of each room.
8. Description of shop program — record of Mr. Randall's work.
9. Report on sewing and cooking activities — 4H Club.
10. Report of Boy Scouts and other clubs.
11. Report of summer school.
12. Report of music program.
13. Report of library, Spanish Club.
14. S.P.M.D.T.U.
15. Mothers' sewing club.
16. List of "carry over" of school into community.

Each member of the committee was asked to check any item in the following list for which they observed specific evidence:

I. Evidence of interest in conservation as shown in: pictures, reading material, charts, collections, vocabulary lists, individual projects, oral discussions and reports, maps, graphs, or diagrams, murals, results from excursions, plants, terrariums, aquariums, projects, children's drawings, books about nature, questions asked by children, pets in the room.

II. Evidence of the use of community resources in: reading, arithmetic, oral discussion, written work, health education, land program, social science, handcraft, care of individual difference, music, creative work, vocabulary work, playground, equipment, games, improvement, science.

III. Effects of these learning situations upon the children's growth: A.D.A., general spirit in the room, voluntary contributions, general interest in work, holding power for boys and girls, play habits, staying to play habits, conversational habits, pupil - teacher relationship, amount of participation, interest in each other, use of school ground on Saturdays and Sundays, interroom visitation before bell rings, facial expression, presence or absence of emotional tensions affecting mental hygiene.

IV. Evidence of the use of county, state, and federal agencies. (Part of the information is in Mrs. Watson's office.) List what you observe and describe.

V. More detailed evidence that individual interests are receiving attention. Name room and incident. Recognition of individual differences, fitting instruction to individuals, hobbies, collections, diaries, handwork, projects, maps, graphs, creative work, individual correspondence.

VI. Evidence that the school is attempting to extend the children's knowledge beyond Nambé. List evidence in each room and describe.

VII. List work habits observed and rate for each room.

VIII. Evidence of: social concern, inquiring mind, creativeness, that individual responsibility is being developed.

IX. Evidence of progress of pupils in skill subjects.

X. Evidence of the interests of parents in this program: contributions of specimens and plants to class work, contributions to noon lunch, contributions to health program, PTA visits of parents, notes from parents, help in building and grading, A.D.A.

XI. Evidence of "carryover" in the community. Talk with children, teachers, parents, if possible. (See records in Mrs. Watson's office.)

The Committee's Report

The members found themselves under the necessity of either (a) remaining in one room all day in order to get an adequate understanding of the room's program and thus failing to see the whole picture or (b) moving about the various rooms but getting an incomplete picture of any one room.

Accordingly, they pooled their observations rather than presenting individual reports. The following report lacks the detailed supporting evidence but gains in weight as representing combined judgment of a group of competent workers in the field of elementary education.

Significant achievements of the school as viewed by the Evaluation Committee:

1. The most vivid and lasting impression was one of cheerfulness and happiness.
2. There is evidence of a sincere attempt to make the work of the classroom meet the needs of the community.
3. The appearance of children in physical well-being, cleanliness, vigor, and vitality was noticeable.
4. The high degree of individual initiative and responsibility

encouraged by teachers and evidenced in all of the activities of children.

5. Children evidenced a strong feeling of "belonging together" which produced a high degree of consideration,
   courtesy, and social sensitivity.

6. The ability of children to express themselves fluently, in-
   telligently, and with conviction about their activities in
   the school and community.

7. The professional attitude and teamwork of the faculty.

8. The effective use made of the resources available to every
   teacher but overlooked in most situations.

9. The use made of services of related agencies such as the
   Soil Conservation Service, Health Department, Agricul-
   tural Extension Service, State Game and Fish Department,
   WPA program, NYA, and other services.

10. The articulateness, interest, curiosity, and critical judg-
    ment evidenced by children, is in the judgment of the
    committee ample evidence of the superiority of child-and-
    community-centered program over the conventional type
    of work.

11. The wide variety of activities sponsored in each room
    evidenced an appreciation of the significance of individual
    differences and a genuine desire to meet them. The at-
    tempt to provide activities of the manual and artistic type
    as well as the linguistic is particularly commended.

12. Responsibility is accorded children in planning the work
    of the classroom, the care of buildings and grounds, and
    activities relating to community activities.

13. The school is successful in enlisting the aid and support
    of parents in supplementing the WPA school lunch proj-
    ect, improving grounds, securing equipment, and conduct-
    ing experimental work in improved agricultural practices.

14. It is the committee's feeling that acquaintance with the
    natural world is being overemphasized to the neglect of

needed preparation in the field of social knowledge and relations.

15. The committee feels that written expression is probably underemphasized.

Signed, COMMITTEE.

Criticism of the Evaluation of March 6, by
Mr. Frank Angel

The staff of the school asked Mr. Frank Angel to reply to the group and to individual criticisms. The first part of the criticism deals with individual remarks, the last part with the committee's report.

I felt that the evaluation had not been thorough enough. I feel that if it had been we would have had more extensive positive comments, perhaps more also on the negative side.

In the first place, the scantiness of critical comment — or better said, of any comment, was evidence to me of the superficiality of observation. Taking each topic which the evaluators were asked to appraise, I want to indicate under each those things which I thought were evident on that day. It seems, also, judging from the reactions, that the evaluators were more concerned with the quantity and physical aspect of the school than with the quality, inasmuch as the observable evidence is indicative of the type and quality of work carried on. Perhaps more time for discussion should have been given.

Evidence of interest in conservation.

Under this heading only the more obvious were tabulated. Some other things and activities which could have been listed are:

a. Reading material (abundance of books, pamphlets, etc.)
b. Vocabulary lists
c. Tree diaries, ant diary

d.   Murals on land use
e.   Plants, roots, mountings
f.   Terrarium
g.   Aquarium
h.   Science books
i.   Discussion on conservation — controlling of watershed

In the same way, each heading was not covered as it could
have been. I failed to locate any, except very cursory remarks
on social concern, inquiring mind, individual responsibility.
Creativeness seemed to be very evident, so this was commented
on.

In addition to the positive comments made by the evaluators,
I would have added the following:

1. From the accumulated evidence, there is a high degree of
    insight and practice in the ways of democracy, particularly
    evident in the respect accorded each individual and the fact
    that each pupil is treated as an individual, as well as the ex-
    tent of "belongingness" evident.

2. That the pupils are well prepared to deal effectively with
    living in other places outside of Nambé, which is evident
    from the way in which the pupils are urged to think critic-
    ally and develop their individual potentialities with due
    regard to other individuals' rights.

3. That community needs and problems are given paramount
    consideration, and at the elementary school level, as much
    is being done to carry out improvement as is possible.
    Where this stops a readiness for expert help is being
    developed in those areas where social improvement and re-
    construction are evident, namely: (a) land use, (b) com-
    munity health, (c) home making.

4. That there is sincere understanding of the difficulties en-
    countered in language by Spanish-speaking youngsters with

meager backgrounds as evidenced by the vocabulary work
being carried on.

5. That an effort is being made to make learning functional
   is evidenced by skill tie-ups.

As rebuttal to the two criticisms, items 14 and 15, given by
the committee, I think both were unwarranted. On the contrary, I believe that a more thorough observation would have
shown evidence that both contentions were wrong.

"Acquaintance with the natural world is being over-empha-
sized to the neglect of needed preparation in the field of social
knowledge and relations."

1. Emphasis on the natural world happened to be purely co-
   incidental as a look at the list of units taught this year and
   previously will show. It could have been argued that because we are in a rural area and much concrete material is
   available, teachers are tempted to use natural science material predominantly. To this, I think can be shown contrary
   evidence. Throughout all levels, excursions, discussions,
   charts, etc., have been developed that show interest in the
   social phase of community life, e.g., to the store, mill, farming activities, garage, wood hauling, land use, Santa Fe,
   transportation — train, wagons, etc. The program is well
   balanced.

Inherent in the committee's criticism is one that the school
should urge more vicarious experiencing. To this it can be
said, we do experience vicariously, but we recognize that vicarious experiences, as such, usually are doubtful and erroneous.
That, therefore, it is our duty to enrich common experiences
in order that a true and correct interpretation of foreign concepts can be given. And that even then there is much room for
doubt as to the interpretation that will be made. We are giving
to the child tools, and are earnestly trying to develop critical

thinking, so his interpretations of vicarious experiences can be more exact.

Inherent also, in the second criticism that writing is probably being underemphasized, is the implication that perhaps the work presented can be at a more mature level (upper grades).

I can think of no more effective retort than, "If we work with children we realize and consider their limitations and possibilities." Mr. ———'s suggestion that more be done in government, voting, etc., may be applicable to more mature groups or I can well imagine elementary children of the Washington, D. C., schools being vitally interested. By the same logic our children are more vitally interested in farming.

Section 1

EVALUATION OF THE 3 R's

Although the Nambé school has emphasized the study of natural science; has given time for the pupils to work on the grounds and gullies, in the shops, in the sewing and cooking room; has emphasized oral language more than written language; has put the development of right habits and attitudes above all else, this program did not exclude the study of the basic skills. On the contrary, as stated in our *Principles of Selection of Subject Matter,* "we shall expect each child to be reasonably proficient in the basic skills of the three R's. . . ."

Table 1 records the results of the Nambé children on the Master Achievement Test used by the county superintendent. These scores are fairly close to the norm. They also give proof that our children absorbed a great deal of geographical data even though we did not teach it directly as a

TABLE 1
1941 Md. Scores, Master Achievement Test

Grade	Sci. & Health	Arith.	Rdg.	Hist.	Eng.	Geog.
8	8.4	8.2	8.3	7.8	7.75	*
7	7.7	7.45	7.85	6.75	6.95	7.25
6	*	*	6.4	*	5.55	*
5	*	*	5.8	*	5.6	*
4	*	*	4.6	*	*	*
3	*	*	3.9	*	*	*
2	*	*	2.7	*	*	*
1	*	*	1.5	*	*	*

* No tests were given.

special subject, but as a part of the social studies. In reading there is a consistent gain from grade to grade, which would seem to indicate that the test really tests the same reading skills which we are teaching in Nambé.

TABLE 2
1941 Md. Scores, Progressive Achievement Tests Nambé School

Grade	R. V.	R. C.	A. R.	A. F.	L.	G. P.	Form A Age
1	1.55	2.4	2.0	0	0	1.55	8
2	2.2	2.6	2.4	0	1.9	2.15	9
3	3.6	4.0	3.2	2.0	3.3	3.0	10
4	4.1	4.5	3.9	3.5	3.7	4.0	11
5	4.65	5.4	4.5	4.0	4.55	4.55	11
6	4.3	5.3	4.7	4.5	4.2	4.6	13
7	6.35	6.35	6.95	7.1	6.9	6.7	14
8	7.25	6.8	7.75	6.75	7.25	7.0	15

Table 2 records the more detailed results of the Nambé children shown on the Progressive Achievement Test. The data should be read as follows: Grade 1 made a median score of 1.55 on reading vocabulary; 2.4 on reading comprehension; 2.0 on arithmetic reasoning; 0 on arithmetic

fundamentals; o on language; and 1.55 on grade placement.
   A study of the data indicates:

   (a) These pupils are lower in reading vocabulary than
in reading comprehension. They are more able to grasp
the general significance of a paragraph and indicate the correct response than to accurately indicate the meaning of
single words isolated from context.

   (b) Reading comprehension is close to, or above, the
normal expectation in the first five grades. The upper three
grades are 1.5 to 2 years below norm. This was not unex-
pected. When we inaugurated the policy of insisting that
every child of school age must attend school, we knew that
this action would bring in many children with low academic background. These large over-age boys and girls had
attended school intermittently. Work and sickness and
more often a lack of interest had raised havoc with basic
skills. There were twenty pupils in 1935 classified in the
fourth grade because of age who were nonreaders. It was
both a source of pride to the staff that our program kept
them in school and a cause for tearing of hair because they
consistently lowered the scores on standard tests (and also
took instructional attention from others who might have
made greater progress).

   (c) In arithmetic reasoning, our children were generally
low, but the arithmetic fundamentals were lower. These
results in grades 1 and 2 are particularly interesting due to
the fact that we gave no formal instruction in arithmetic in
these grades. The fact that they did so well in the primary
grades on arithmetic reasoning is probably due to their

ability to read, since the problems were of the narrative type. If this reasoning be true, it would be anticipated that the upper graders, who were poor readers, would be below on arithmetic reasoning.

(d) In language, the children were uniformly low. This would be expected in light of our philosophy. We felt that the oral aspect of language is much more important *in our situation* than written language. The test emphasized the mechanical side of written language: capitalization, punctuation, spelling, handwriting.

(e) The grade placement is a composite score, and since the medians are low in arithmetic and language, the grade placements are accordingly low.

(f) Summary. When these results were studied by the staff, we felt that the results indicated that the pupils were not "reasonably proficient" in arithmetic, especially in the fundamentals. Accordingly, all teachers above the first grade agreed to put more emphasis on this subject. The time allotment in the schedule appeared ample, so it seemed

TABLE 3
1942 Md. Scores for the Nambé School on the Progressive
Achievement Tests

Grade	R. V.	R. C.	A. R.	A. F.	L.	G. P.	Age
1	1.7	2.4	2.0	1.8	2.1	2.2	7
2	3.1	3.75	3.05	2.6	2.95	2.85	9
3	3.75	4.2	3.65	3.0	3.55	3.55	10
4	4.1	4.7	4.35	4.1	4.2	4.20	11
5	4.5	4.35	4.55	4.6	5.05	4.75	11.5
6	5.5	6.45	5.9	5.55	5.75	5.70	12
7	4.4	5.3	4.95	5.0	4.5	4.7	14
8	6.2	6.6	7.7	7.2	6.5	6.80	15

to be a matter of more forceful teaching rather than a mere increase in class recitation.

Table 3 presents the results in May, 1942, as shown by the Progressive Achievement Test. It will be noted that in arithmetic reasoning (A.R.), arithmetic fundamentals (A.F.), and in language (L.), there was a gain over 1941 in every grade through the first six grades. The only exception was where the 1941 score was very high. This gain was secured at no cost to the reading program. Evidently the greater attention by the teachers in these subjects brought results.

It is also interesting to note that the Nursery School is showing its value. For the first time the median age of the first graders is seven years. Inasmuch as these non-English-speaking youngsters must attend the prefirst room for one year to learn English, the age of seven is considered normal. This is promising for the future. It also presents evidence that when the conditions of learning are made equal, native Spanish-speaking children can be expected to make as normal progress as any group.

The upper grades were low when we began, are low now and will remain low until the group of academically deficient children, previously mentioned, is eliminated. In reporting the data and computing the medians we included every child classified in the particular grade. For example, the present seventh grade had a G. P. (grade placement) of 4.7 on the 1942 Progressive Achievement Test. Had we dropped the ones who were seventh graders "in name only," the G. P. would have been higher. This situation was one

of our justifications for introducing such a varied program
—land management, crafts, music, etc.

The point might be raised, "If you had given the time to
the basic skills that you spend on the 'extra' subjects, perhaps your G. P. would have been higher." To this we would
say:

(1) That we did try very hard to teach the basic skills
to these youngsters. Special classes were formed for them,
but three years was not long enough to resuscitate lost interests and cover the work of seven normal years.

(2) Had it not been for the flavor given to the daily program by the "extra" subjects these children would not have
remained in school. Their interest in academic work was
too low to hold them. The main problem was to keep them
in school and help them to learn as much as possible. One
boy who is still unable to read much more than a first
reader made chairs for the home, a clock shelf, and painted
a picture that the mother points to with pride and joy. He
has risen in the esteem of the neighborhood; he has some
self-confidence and in general will be a better citizen than if
he had been dropped from school as a complete failure.
Shall the school be for the child or the child for the school?

Section 2

EVALUATION OF THE NATURAL SCIENCE PROGRAM

Our Guiding Principles make it clear that the Nambé
school would devote a great deal of attention to natural
science and in particular land management. The chapters
describing the work of individual rooms show how this sub-

ject was woven into the curriculum. It became necessary then to find out if our children knew more about land management than the pupils of other county schools. It also was necessary to find out whether this emphasis might cause the Nambé children to be lower in the customary school subjects than the children of the other schools.

Since there was no land management test available, we made one with the help of the experts in the education division of the Soil Conservation Service. It consisted of four parts.

Part I was composed of fifty words or terms whose understanding is necessary for intelligent reading. Each word is followed by several answers from which the correct answer is selected.

Example: Silt means — silver, fine earth, skin, secure, cloth.

Land contours run — up and down hill, around a slope, in triangles, in squares, in politics.

Part II consisted of one hundred statements in true or false arrangement:

Examples: The slowing down of the water is of great importance in erosion control.

Land should have only as much livestock as its carrying capacity permits.

Forest fires aid ground cover.

Part III was made up of ten sentences in completion form with the correct answers to be selected from a list of twenty-five answers at the bottom of the page.

Examples: Vegetated . . . . . . will help control floods.
A steady crop of trees from our forest is called . . . .
(Answers not given here for lack of space.)

Part IV was composed of (a) nine pictures of common
plants which had to be identified by some characteristic
feature and three pictures to be interpreted.

Examples: Pictures of rabbit bush, side oats grama, and
blue grama. (b) three diagrams with items to be identified.

Example: A soil profile. Pupil must name the different
parts.

No scientific precision is claimed for the test, but it did
seem to include the crucial material. It furthermore tested
both a knowledge of the principles dealing with land management and the ability to apply these principles. Whatever
errors were inherent in the test should apply equally to all
the schools tested.

This test was given to the eighth grade class in Nambé

TABLE 4
APRIL, 1941, MD. SCORES LAND MANAGEMENT TEST

School	Age	Vocabulary	Technical Terms	Application	Comprehension	Total
School A	14	25.5	23	3	12	58.5
School B	15	31	20.5	4	12.5	70.5
School C	14	30.5	32	3	10	73
Nambé	15	37	41	6.5	17.5	104

and three other schools of the county. In one there had been regular instruction in the subject under the same general coöperation with the Soil Conservation Service as we had enjoyed. In the other two schools only a limited amount of incidental instruction had been given.

It appears from Table 4 that the Nambé children did significantly better work on all sections of the test than the children of the other schools.

Since some aspect of natural science, including land management, is developed in every grade at Nambé, there should be a gradual accretion of knowledge as the pupils progress from the lower to higher grades. Theoretically this suggests that successive eight grades should make better responses on the test. However, as we had only one form, we were unable to verify this hypothesis.

To ascertain if the gain in knowledge of land management was secured at the expense of other subjects, we compared the results of a test administered by the county superintendent to all county schools. Table 5 presents the data for schools taking the Land Management Test. (School A was a municipal school and did not take the test.)

While there are some variations, the most striking feature is the close general resemblance of the three schools as measured by this test.

It appears then that the Nambé program was as effective as other schools in teaching usual academic subjects and in addition, enabled the pupils to learn considerably more about one of their most valuable assets — the land.

One of the most striking accomplishments in Nambé

TABLE 5
Comparison of Grade Mds. of Nambé, School B, and School C on the Master Achievement Test, April and May, 1941

Grade	Nambé						School B						School C					
	Rdg.	Eng.	Sci. & Health	Arith.	Geog.	Hist.	Rdg.	Eng.	Sci. & Health	Arith.	Geog.	Hist.	Rdg.	Eng.	Sci. & Health	Arith.	Geog.	Hist.
1	1.5	—	—	—	—	—	1.3	—	—	—	—	—	1.6	—	—	—	—	—
2	2.7	—	—	—	—	—	2.8	—	—	—	—	—	2.8	—	—	—	—	—
3	3.9	—	—	—	—	—	3.7	—	—	—	—	—	3.9	—	—	—	—	—
4	4.6	—	—	—	—	—	5.1	—	—	—	—	—	4.65	—	—	—	—	—
5	5.8	5.6	—	—	—	—	3.85	4.15	—	—	—	—	5.5	5.65	—	—	—	—
6	6.4	5.5	—	—	—	—	6.6	6.1	—	—	—	—	6.9	6.8	—	—	—	—
7	7.85	6.95	7.7	7.45	7.25	6.75	7.85	7.5	8.3	7.55	7.35	7.25	7.3	7.1	7.2	7.5	7.1	7.1
8	8.3	7.25	8.4	8.2	—	7.8	8.4	8.5	8.45	8.5	7.9	8.45	8.8	9.0	8.2	8.9	—	9.6

was the change in *attitude* toward land and water resources. Not only did the children realize that land was their basic resource from which stem food, shelter, clothing, and other necessities, but they realized *their* responsibility to the land. Nor did they think in terms only of *their* school grounds, or *their* field, but of the interaction of natural forces and the interdependence of human beings, i. e., that mismanagement of the watershed causes destruction to fields below — that one man's misuse of land affects the land of another — that gullies and floods are not stopped by man's fences or boundaries or ownership.

Section 3

EVALUATION — AVERAGE DAILY ATTENDANCE

The average daily attendance of a school is always studied in a school survey. Its significance arises from the fact that it indicates the extent of attendance. The enrollment figures may give a false impression, since that number represents the total number of different people entering the school during the year. Some children might be there only a few days. The A. D. A., if honestly reported, tells the number of pupils who are in school day by day. Its importance is recognized in all formulas for distribution of public money to individual systems.

Table 6 gives the enrollment for the four years from 1937-38 to 1940-41. The 29 per cent increase in enrollment in four years was doubtless due to many factors.

One of the outstanding accomplishments was the increased interest in education on the part of both parents

TABLE 6
ENROLLMENT OF THE NAMBÉ SCHOOL

1937-38	Sept. 30	Feb. 28
Pupils enrolled	180	185
Number dropped	8	11
Net enrollment	172	174
Average daily attendance	159.4	167
1938-39		
Pupils enrolled	188	215
Number dropped	4	5
Net enrollment	184	210
Average daily attendance	166.31	195.42
1939-40		
Pupils enrolled	220	232
Number dropped	0	13
Net enrollment	220	219
Average daily attendance	205.3	212
1940-41		
Pupils enrolled	217	230
Number dropped	0	11
Net enrollment	217	219
Average daily attendance	206.55	214.25

and children. Fathers could see the value of a program that taught the boys how to improve their farms. They ceased to keep the boys out for trivial jobs. Sometimes they hired help. At other times arrangements were made to excuse boys early in the afternoon.

The children liked to come to school and "playing hookey" was unusual. This interest was instrumental in changing the attitude of some parents toward attendance. A few instances came to our attention of grandparents who sent to other villages for grandchildren in order that they could attend the Nambé school. One or two families moved into the village because of the reputation of the school.

Perhaps the per cent of attendance each year is the most amazing fact shown in Table 6. The per cent of attendance

varies from 90-93 per cent. This is a very high figure for a
rural school. In New Mexico as a whole, the per cent of
attendance among rural children for the school year of
1936-37 was 76. Again, the interest of the children worked
to prevent minor absences. The work of the nurse and general attention to health on the part of all teachers played
its part. The hot lunch program helped. Certainly the
energetic policy of the staff was effective. If the cause of a
child's absence was unknown, someone visited the home
that evening!

Whatever the reason, each day saw the majority of our
children trudging to school in rain, snow, mud, or dust.
And many a day the first task was to dry off before attempting instruction. These data present positive evidence that
Spanish-speaking parents will take the same interest in
schooling and make the same sacrifices as any other parents
when they feel that their children are getting value received.

Section 4

EVALUATION OF ATTITUDES

An evaluation program which stops with the measure-
ment of the three R's has missed the most valuable
learnings which take place in the school. The attitudes,
appreciations and interests which the child has acquired
will probably determine how much of the three R's he re-
members or uses.

The following four attributes were selected for evaluation: (a) social concern, (b) inquiring mind, (c) creative-

ness, (d) development of individual responsibility. These are qualities which are difficult to measure and we had no scientific instrument. The teachers were asked to make a record of every instance which they observed involving these four attributes. A brief list of observed acts may have some value, for it is logical that such acts are not the accidental occurrences of just one day, but must grow with the development of the child. Once a habit or an attitude is established it becomes more than an incidental happening. The following incidents were selected from many pages of similar ones; many others passed unnoted.

Social Concern: From the time a child enters school he is a social individual and is responsible for certain acts which can improve or aid the social behavior and well-being of his group. Good citizenship is social concern.

. . . . . .

Pablo, emerging from the toilet with two small boys said, "They were not using the toilet in the right way."

. . . . . .

Abelino was working in the shop. He came in with a broken coping saw blade (in itself evidence of growth, for as a general rule if a blade is broken, it is left on the bench and later everyone disclaims knowledge of it). He wished another. It was during practice for the Christmas program. He came back minus the blade, saying, "I didn't want to bother Mrs. Watson, she was busy practicing the program."

. . . . . .

Idalia said, "Mrs. Sanchez, the windows need washing. I know of a way to clean them easily. At home we use kerosene to clean the panes, then we wipe them with a clean cloth."

. . . . . .

Jose noted that the rain was rushing across the school grounds and none was running into the pit around the trees. He asked permission to go out and make a new trench so the water would flow to the trees.

. . . . . .

Inquiring Mind: The pupil who asks questions, seeks information and tries experiments will gain more than the passive and inert one. No doubt the attitude of the teacher will encourage or discourage this characteristic.

During a discussion on speed, Librado said, "I have watched to see if I can see the bullet when it comes out of the rifle. I haven't seen any, I guess they go too fast."

. . . . . .

Santiago reported that he had caught a small bluish-gray bird. He fed it after he examined it to see if it was all right. He then turned it loose. He went to the bookcases and looked in different books until he found a picture which fitted the description of the bird.

. . . . . .

Sostenes had caught a stray ant from the ant nest. He was examining it. Finally he brought it up to me saying, "Look where the ant has its eyes. It also has little pliers." Later, I saw him looking at ant pictures in the science books.

. . . . . .

Abelino was writing a sentence with the word "years." Upon checking it, I found he had written: "Columbus came to America 449 years ago." I asked where he had read that. He answered, "I didn't read it, I worked it out."

. . . . . .

Creativeness: Thinking is not stimulated by reading and "figuring" alone. Children must have opportunity to work with paints, with wood, with soil, and plants in order that the skills may be used as tools for the development of their individual responsibility in planning and building. This not only broadens the academic program for average boys and girls, but provides richer learning experiences for the superior pupils.

Adela had been working on a report telling what happens to food in the body. She had been puzzling for some time as to how to present her material to the group. Today I noticed she had glued two tagboards together and had placed Irene against them and traced her. She cut the shape out and began cutting shapes of digestive organs to put in the body.

. . . . . .

I saw Natividad placing pieces of paper on Dora's back. Later I asked what was going on. Natividad had made a paper pattern for Dora to use in making a dress.

. . . . . .

Many new projects have been started during the last two weeks: Tranquilino and Nestor are making a table from reeds, Benancio is making a bird house from scraps to take home, Jose is carving a wall decoration and is working on a Chinese checker game to take home, Tony is making a large chair for his home, Joe made two small stands for holding saints. He worked out his own designs. Antonio designed and made two candlesticks out of wood. Dora made a runner for the radio. She also carved an all-over design and is block printing it. Emma and Virginia are block printing table-runners.

Individual Responsibility: If responsibility is to be assumed there must first be recognition of the need for it. Secondly there must be opportunities for practice. The teacher-pupil relationships in Nambé were based upon planning together, sharing tasks, and accepting responsibilities.

Erminio spilled the water during handwashing. He started a very inefficient job of mopping. Bobbie went over to him, finished the mopping and, when Erminio was asked to take the mop back to the kitchen, said, "But I want to mop up the water around the bucket after we finish washing."

.   .   .   .   .   .

Odulia knew we planned to send specimens of Indian pottery to Australia. Although she was not the one delegated to do so, she brought a small box full of pieces today. She said, "I have saved these for a long time, but I think it is all right to send them to Australia."

.   .   .   .   .   .

While I was busy at the circle, Mr. Lujan knocked on the door. Usually Celina answers but today she was absent. After waiting a few minutes to see if I would ask someone else, which I didn't do, Librado rose, went to the door and then called me.

.   .   .   .   .   .

Willie was walking to lunch with me. I complimented him on the progress he was making in reading. He said, "I want to learn to read well. My father wanted me to stay home and work today. I told him I could do the work after school this afternoon."

.   .   .   .   .   .

Maria felt that the boys were not doing a very good job of collecting the grass seed. She said she would harvest them by herself.

Section 5

EVALUATION OF OTHER PHASES

It is logical that the program of a community school, based upon the immediate needs of the community, would have some effect upon the living conditions and practices of the people in the community. Yet we cannot definitely state how much was or was not accomplished. At times the results were obvious, at other times the only hint of impending change was the slow growth of wholesome and progressive attitudes on the part of the people. We do not feel the effects which are listed here are all inclusive. But they constitute some definite accomplishments.

Clothing

In homes where money is scarce and is made the hard way it is not surprising that the clothes will be old and worn. Yet one of the invariable comments of visitors was, "What happy children, how clean and well-dressed they are." The school, naturally, cannot claim all the credit. But during the five years there was a growing pride, on the part of the children, in their appearance: hair that once hung loose and blown was neatly braided; faces were scrubbed and ears were washed. The older girls began to use less make-up, and lipstick on nine and ten-year-olds disappeared entirely. Sewing classes were established during the first year and the school was helped by the able coöperation of the home extension agent. Girls in the upper grades learned to use patterns and sew, they gave style shows and high heels were discarded for flat-heeled school shoes. A pattern library was established and patterns were checked out for the use of the mothers in the community. During the last three years of the program it was possible to conduct regular classes in sewing for the older girls. This was due to the leadership of Mrs. Ford, the first grade teacher. After finishing her regular classes she conducted food and serving classes and classes where the girls learned to make over clothes and to make new dresses of attractive and practical materials.

During one summer vacation, Mrs. Ford remained in Nambé, conducting sewing and cooking classes for the mothers and older girls. The women learned to use patterns, buy materials and to launder them without fading the colors. Frequently during the year several women from the community would come in after school to use the sewing machines or go to one of the teachers' homes for help in laying out a pattern or cutting out a dress. The extensive use of the pattern library was, in itself, evidence that the women were making use of the opportunities offered.

Diet in the Homes

It is a slow process to change people's food habits. Often it is a matter of changing the economic situation and then changes in the diet follow.

Due to the influence of the school nurse, the foods class conducted by the school, the school lunches and the classroom programs, there were some changes in diet. The people became aware of the importance of fresh fruit and vegetables; the older girls learned to prepare common food

in a variety of ways and received recipes which they tested
and took home to use:

At home I have made every recipe we have had in food class.
My mother uses them too. I read them to her in Spanish be-
cause she doesn't read English. — Edalia Garduno, Food Class,
Nambé.

In another instance the girls were amazed to learn that
whole wheat flour could be used in cooking. The children
learned to eat certain foods in the Nursery School and at
the school lunches and demanded them at home. Such
foods as cereal, cooked fruits, and soups were favorites, as
were fresh fruits and vegetables. During the last week of
school the staff was invited to dinner in two different
homes. In each home the meal had been planned and
served with the assistance of the daughters, members of the
eighth grade foods class. The menu consisted of meat,
potatoes, gravy, three different vegetables, salad, fresh fruit,
cake, and coffee.

Canning was better established in the community and
the people became aware of the value of community products such as cooked apples and wheat breakfast food which
could be ground at the local mill. Milk and milk drinks
were great favorites.

Leisure Time

There was little reading in Nambé when the project
program was inaugurated. As the school secured attractive
books and stressed reading it was natural that the children

would take books home. The parents enjoyed reading
these books with the children, or having the children read
to them. We also collected and sent magazines to the
homes. Books from the city library were checked out from
the school library by both children and parents. As the
children learned to use newspapers for current events we
found that a few parents subscribed to a newspaper. As
the war drew nearer to the people of the community they
became very interested in the maps which the school used.
In one grade, three books of political maps were worn out
from constant home and school use.

The children checked out games to take home, and as
they mastered the rules, the older children made games for
family use.

Living Conditions

The effect of the health program has been discussed in
detail in Chapter V. However, the following examples of
better sanitation were noted: three wells were screened,
two WPA toilets were purchased and a few old ones were
relocated. Two households dug trash pits in which to dis-
pose of ashes and tin cans rather than throw them into
some arroyo. In addition to these, there were instances of
other improved home living conditions: ten families installed electric lights; several pieces of handmade furniture,
such as cabinets, cribs, and chairs, were taken into the
homes. One parent took up carpentry, purchased power
tools and made, in addition to other things, a bedstead for
each of his three small daughters.

The School Ground Laboratories

When the Nambé project opened, the playgrounds were covered with puncture vine or bernot. A few Siberian pea shrubs were growing along the south fence, a few Chinese elm trees and some very small walnut saplings were along the north fence. With diligent use of the hoe the puncture vine was eliminated and in 1938 we planted over a hundred Chinese elm trees. In spite of dry seasons every tree lived; others were planted and we now have 275 trees. Each year the boys pruned the trees carefully and new symmetrical crowns developed. The prunings were placed in a gully near the school. Several evergreens, such as Douglas fir, white fir, spruce, and junipers were transplanted from the mountains to the school grounds.

Nearly a hundred small terraces around the margin of the school ground were built for laboratory plots where drought-resistant plants were grown. Native New Mexico grasses were used, such as blue grama, side oats grama, western and crested wheat, and western broom. These small terraces served many purposes. The children learned how to check the rapid runoff on a slope; which plants would hold the terrace walls together with a firm root system; that the good edible grasses could be reëstablished; that water, ordinarily wasted, could be saved. In short, these plots were the laboratories for our natural science classes and, in general, served the same functions as any laboratory. In addition to the terraces, a five-acre piece of ground on Mr. McCormick's property was fenced in for the use of the land management classes. The pupils saw how overgrazed land could be restored under proper management. As the attitude of the adults changed from skepticism to that of admiring co-workers, many asked for grass seeds and cuttings. Several trees were planted at homes and care was taken to divert all the surface runoff toward the newly-planted trees. Many small gullies and one or two large ones were stabilized. More emphasis was placed on growing tomatoes. Seed that matured early (the frost came soon in this altitude) was introduced in the experimental plots. When these plants produced usable fruit the parents were eager to use the same seed.

Epilogue

In the Elizabethan theater it was the custom for one of the actors to appear before the audience at the close of the presentation and confidentially comment on the moral of the play and the manner in which the players walked the stage. So, without benefit of make-up or lights, let the moral of our drama be drawn.

While our work in Nambé has been, at times, both a tragedy and comedy, it partakes of the nature of a historical drama in that it is history in the making and as such merits the thoughtful consideration of all clear-thinking citizens who are concerned with the part the school should play in the community.

On the basis of the principles set up at the initiation of the project, we have demonstrated that a curriculum can be successfully built around the needs of a community; that children can learn from the shop, the land, and the clinic without loss in the formal subjects.

From our experience, then, we are justified in making the suggestion that all of the rural schools of New Mexico should consider a modification of customary curricula if our people are to derive the greatest benefit from their schools. When the government finds it necessary to spend millions each year in New Mexico to save the soil, the

schools are shortsighted indeed if they fail to contribute to
the improvement of the living habits of the people who
are born and die on this land. The intimate relationship
between the economic level and the educational level is
universally recognized. But we have not realized that rural
schools must contribute more than they do to the solution
of the economic problem.

With more than 50 per cent of adults in the United
States having less than an eighth grade schooling, it is no
wonder that it has been necessary to set up so many
agencies to carry on adult education.

We have found that the rural school can do something
to combat superstition and traditional malpractices. We
have seen how much can be done to improve community
health when the public health nurse does not have to
spread her services too thin. And we have had demonstrated again how quickly old habits reassert themselves
when the pressure of the nurse is withdrawn.

Our study at Nambé suggests that if the rural schools
would give less attention to college preparatory courses
and more attention to the problems of their community,
that children would not drop out in large numbers at an
early age and thus be deprived of needed training. It also
shows very clearly that "over age" boys and girls will remain in school under certain circumstances; that they can
be made happy; that they can be developed into responsible beings; and that they can learn ways of improving
health and living conditions even though they fail to make
the customary academic progress.

It has been surprising to discover the large number of agencies that are at hand to help us and somewhat disconcerting to realize that these have grown up because we as a people have lost the ability or are unable to solve our own problems. We ask very seriously, "Does this situation exist because of social and economic forces beyond our control or have we bungled the educational program somewhere, and are we now on the wrong road?"

We realize that some of the benefits of the Nambé school were achieved because private philanthropy made it possible to spend more money for school purposes than the ordinary county budget permits. Other schools might realize the same objectives under the same circumstances.

The question, then, is whether a program such as has been developed at Nambé justifies the expenditure of so much money. If it does, should not the state or federal government invest similar sums in all rural schools in order that other communities may receive like benefits?

The experience at Nambé has taught us that the influence of an elementary school is limited. A little child may know what is the correct care for the land or a sick brother, but custom and parental authority outweigh him. — No, we feel confident that had we possessed a high school at Nambé in which the same kind of instruction could have continued that was initiated in the grades, that progress would have been much greater. For example, with a high school we could have had a full-time teacher of agriculture, one who could have gone with the boys to the farms and actually initiated changed practices. In a high school homemaking department the older girls might have learned more habits which would have been put into immediate practice.

It is reasonable to expect that more boys and girls would have continued in school if a high school with similar ideals controlled by us had been located at Nambé. But if a child goes from an elementary school where the emphasis is on thinking to a formal high school where the emphasis is on memory, he is a misfit. He must adjust himself to the new situation or fail. That is actually what happened to our eighth graders. Some refused to conform and dropped out of the high school they attended. A few adjusted themselves and looked askance at their previous training. This in turn reacted on parents and the younger brothers and sisters who were still at Nambé, and naturally lessened their confidence in our work. But any new idea inevitably meets opposition.

As brought out in the chapter on "community coöperation," the program developed more completely as teachers and the community learned to work together. Every change in the staff retarded the program in the particular room involved until the new teacher became acquainted with the program, the needs of the pupils and the community.

Five years look like a long time, but when social change is concerned they are "as a passing shadow." When the original plans were made it was suggested that probably no real changes in community habits and attitudes would be measurable in five years. Such proved the case. The data presented in Chapter VII show clearly that the staff of the school was just beginning to get the school properly organized. The children in the lower grades were just reaching a satisfactory academic level. One can only wonder what they might have done had they continued. Progress must be measured in generations, not years.

These years of work at Nambé reënforce our opinion that it is wrong to make special categories for Spanish-speaking people as though they were quite different from all other groups. It is true that the language makes a complication; that past generations make for different social customs — but in the essentials of life people are pretty much alike anywhere you find them. As we place children in equally favorable environments they tend to react very much alike. Improve the economic level of rural New Mexico, give boys and girls schooling that will help them solve their own problems, and by so doing we build a better state.

THE CHICANO HERITAGE

An Arno Press Collection

Adams, Emma H. **To and Fro in Southern California.** 1887

Anderson, Henry P. **The Bracero Program in California.** 1961

Aviña, Rose Hollenbaugh. **Spanish and Mexican Land Grants in California.** 1976

Barker, Ruth Laughlin. **Caballeros.** 1932

Bell, Horace. **On the Old West Coast.** 1930

Biberman, Herbert. **Salt of the Earth.** 1965

Casteñeda, Carlos E., trans. **The Mexican Side of the Texas Revolution (1836).** 1928

Casteñeda, Carlos E. **Our Catholic Heritage in Texas, 1519-1936.** Seven volumes. 1936-1958

Colton, Walter. **Three Years in California.** 1850

Cooke, Philip St. George. **The Conquest of New Mexico and California.** 1878

Cue Canovas, Agustin. **Los Estados Unidos Y El Mexico Olvidado.** 1970

Curtin, L. S. M. **Healing Herbs of the Upper Rio Grande.** 1947

Fergusson, Harvey. **The Blood of the Conquerors.** 1921

Fernandez, Jose. **Cuarenta Años de Legislador:** Biografia del Senador Casimiro Barela. 1911

Francis, Jessie Davies. **An Economic and Social History of Mexican California** (1822-1846). Volume I: Chiefly Economic. Two vols. in one. 1976

Getty, Harry T. **Interethnic Relationships in the Community of Tucson.** 1976

Guzman, Ralph C. **The Political Socialization of the Mexican American People.** 1976

Harding, George L. **Don Agustin V. Zamorano.** 1934

Hayes, Benjamin. **Pioneer Notes from the Diaries of Judge Benjamin Hayes, 1849-1875.** 1929

Herrick, Robert. **Waste.** 1924

Jamieson, Stuart. **Labor Unionism in American Agriculture.** 1945

Landolt, Robert Garland. **The Mexican-American Workers of San Antonio, Texas.** 1976

Lane, Jr., John Hart. **Voluntary Associations Among Mexican Americans in San Antonio, Texas.** 1976

Livermore, Abiel Abbot. **The War with Mexico Reviewed.** 1850

Loyola, Mary. **The American Occupation of New Mexico, 1821-1852.** 1939

Macklin, Barbara June. **Structural Stability and Culture Change in a Mexican-American Community.** 1976

McWilliams, Carey. **Ill Fares the Land:** Migrants and Migratory Labor in the United States. 1942

Murray, Winifred. **A Socio-Cultural Study of 118 Mexican Families Living in a Low-Rent Public Housing Project in San Antonio, Texas.** 1954

Niggli, Josephina. **Mexican Folk Plays.** 1938

Parigi, Sam Frank. **A Case Study of Latin American Unionization in Austin, Texas.** 1976

Poldervaart, Arie W. **Black-Robed Justice.** 1948

Rayburn, John C. and Virginia Kemp Rayburn, eds. **Century of Conflict, 1821-1913.** Incidents in the Lives of William Neale and William A. Neale, Early Settlers in South Texas. 1966

Read, Benjamin. **Illustrated History of New Mexico.** 1912

Rodriguez, Jr., Eugene. **Henry B. Gonzalez.** 1976

Sanchez, Nellie Van de Grift. **Spanish and Indian Place Names of California.** 1930

Sanchez, Nellie Van de Grift. **Spanish Arcadia.** 1929

Shulman, Irving. **The Square Trap.** 1953

Tireman, L. S. **Teaching Spanish-Speaking Children.** 1948

Tireman, L. S. and Mary Watson. **A Community School in a Spanish-Speaking Village.** 1948

Twitchell, Ralph Emerson. **The History of the Military Occupation of the Territory of New Mexico.** 1909

Twitchell, Ralph Emerson. **The Spanish Archives of New Mexico.** Two vols. 1914

U. S. House of Representatives. **California and New Mexico:** Message from the President of the United States, January 21, 1850. 1850

Valdes y Tapia, Daniel. **Hispanos and American Politics.** 1976

West, Stanley A. **The Mexican Aztec Society.** 1976

Woods, Frances Jerome. **Mexican Ethnic Leadership in San Antonio, Texas.** 1949

Aspects of the Mexican American Experience. 1976

Mexicans in California After the U. S. Conquest. 1976

Hispanic Folklore Studies of Arthur L. Campa. 1976

Hispano Culture of New Mexico. 1976

Mexican California. 1976

The Mexican Experience in Arizona. 1976

The Mexican Experience in Texas. 1976

Mexican Migration to the United States. 1976

The United States Conquest of California. 1976

Northern Mexico On the Eve of the United States Invasion:
Rare Imprints Concerning California, Arizona, New Mexico,
and Texas, 1821-1846. Edited by David J. Weber. 1976